Dr. Carey's® Baby Care

Written by Carey Chronis, M.D.
Published by Dr. Carey's® January 2014

ISBN: 978-0-9913417-0-2

MW00439172

Every reasonable effort has been made to confirm the accuracy of the information herein, however, when it comes to medical information, reasonable minds sometimes differ and standards of practice can vary from region to region. In addition, information does change and errors do occur. In that regard, we welcome comments, criticism and, above all, notification regarding errors or omissions. Please send us your comments to the address below. The reader is expected to use the contents of this book as source of information only. The contents of *Dr. Carey's® Baby Care: First Year Baby Care Guide*, is not a substitute for advice from a qualified physician. It is important to consult your baby's physician prior to starting medical treatment. The reader is also expected to consult the package insert for appropriate guidelines and use of any therapeutic or pharmaceutical agent recommended in this book prior to instituting treatment.

Dr. Carey's®
1746-F South Victoria Avenue, #307
Ventura, California 93003

Acknowledgements

A project of this scope does not happen by chance and does not occur in a vacuum. Countless people have generously given me their time and input to help make my dream a reality. Special thanks go to my daughter, Claire, for her continued support. Stan Whisenhunt, Joan Phelps and Jake Finch of Whisenhunt Communications have all knocked themselves out to help shape my vision and Vas Smountas for brining new life to our look. In addition, my wonderful staff and very patient patients have been incredibly generous in lending their time and their images in my pursuit of the perfect picture. Thank you to all for their continued support. Lastly, thanks to my mom and Lou for all of their helpful suggestions, and to my dad, who I dearly miss.

Introduction

I've wanted to be a doctor since I was in the ninth grade. When I told a family friend who was an orthopedic surgeon that I was interested in medicine, he arranged for me to watch a surgery he performed on a patient's knee.

The knee was prepped and wrapped. I'm standing there gowned and excited. The doctor makes the first cut, I see the bone glistening at me, and I hit the floor. But, I wasn't deterred. I went back in to watch a second surgery and I was hooked. From that point on, I was going to become a doctor.

When I was in medical school, I hit my pediatric rotation during my third year and found my calling. I loved working with children and their families. The children were fun, the parents were fun, everything was fun. I liked the fast pace. It was right for me. There was always something different going on. It changed every ten minutes. The noises didn't bother me. It was all good.

When it came to working with the parents, the questions they asked were great. I liked explaining things to a child who was old enough to understand, but I also liked explaining things to the parent who was the healthy subject in the conversation. It's great to get that connection.

I learned very quickly that parents need to be on board with what's going on with their children. And, when possible, the child needs to be on board too. One of the fun things I do in my office when the child is there is I ask him or her all of the questions. Or, if a brother or sister is in there too, I'll ask one child what's going on with the other. It's fun to watch their faces when you make them the center of the world.

This was where the idea for this book was born. There were so many questions that parents, especially new parents, ask when they come to see me. As physicians specializing in children and pediatric healthcare, we see the stages of development slip by so quickly that sometimes we gloss over those important moments and small miracles when the parents ask about them. There's a rash? It will pass. Your baby isn't babbling yet? Don't worry, it will happen. It's easy to dismiss the parents' question or concern because we know the topic is fleeting. But, we physicians do know the nuances, reasons and details behind most of the stages, phases and minor issues you and your baby will encounter. I know, as a parent, that it's important for other parents to have these milestones explained to them.

> **There were so many questions that parents, especially new parents, ask when they come to see me.**

Think of this book as a user's guide to your baby's first year, an office visit to your baby's physician found between the covers of this book. It's arranged so that the most common questions are handled by topic. My goal is to answer a lot of the questions parents have that their own physicians may not spend the time to really answer, and to do so clearly and simply, and with lots and lots of pictures where appropriate. There are certainly many medically related questions that are best answered by someone in the medical field, but rarely do health practitioners take the time to go into those answers with enough depth for the parents.

Know also that I'm not here to judge you and the decisions you make for your baby. There are as many ways to care for your baby as there are babies. My goal isn't to have people raise their children as I've raised my child. I want parents to do what feels comfortable for their family dynamics, but to do so with the information they need to make their choices.

The content of this book will help you handle some of the most common issues that will arise with your baby. Of course, my explanations are not going to cover every possible concern that will present itself. But many of the most routine things you will encounter as parents, (fussy infants, stuffy noses, diaper rashes and so on) can be addressed.

Lastly, I want you all to know that as a parent of a beautiful daughter, I've put to practice all of the tips and techniques I offer to you. Claire, my wonderful daughter, survived her infancy and babyhood with me, and I also survived as well. I can't help but think how blessed I was to have the knowledge I needed to make informed decisions and take action with her. I'm hoping that armed with the same information, you will be a confident parent as well.

Carey Chronis, M.D.

Table of Contents

Chapter 1

Development

Look at What My Baby Did!

Who can't stare at a newborn for hours? Their facial features are so delicate and their smiles are instantly endearing. And, if the baby is yours, she's even more wonderful! Let's look more closely at the milestones that make a baby's development so amazing.

Before we venture down this road, remember that your baby is a one-of-a-kind miracle. Newborns do not read books on child development. They go their own way and at their own pace. While we, as doting parents, keep looking ahead, my wish for you is to stop and savor what your baby is doing now. Their changes happen so fast, you can miss these moments.

• •

Newborn Reflexes

Before babies make "coo" sounds and roll over, they start life with an amazing array of reflexes. Reflexes are involuntary movements that occur time and time again when prompted by your actions.

Rooting and Sucking Reflex

What better way to demonstrate when you want to eat than by having a set of reflexes devoted to eating? By thirty-five weeks gestation, a baby's rooting and sucking reflexes are set. If you lightly stroke your newborn's cheek you'll see his mouth open as he turns his head toward the object (your fingers). This is rooting. If he gets a chance to latch on, he will vigorously suck your fingers. It seems so simple!

Lightly stroking your newborn's cheek causes her mouth to open as she turns her head to the object.

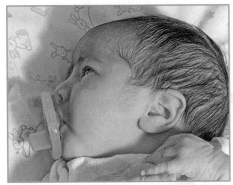

By thirty-five weeks gestation, a baby's rooting and sucking reflexes are set.

Hand and Foot Grasp

This is my favorite reflex. The significance mystifies me, but the hands and feet grasp are the cutest reflexes imaginable, especially with the feet. If you place your extended finger in the palm of your newborn's hand, her tiny fingers will grasp your finger with amazing strength. Similarly, if you place your thumb on her foot just below the toes, your baby's toes will curl. If you try this, I guarantee you can't help but smile. Enjoy it now because her hand grasp disappears by three months of age and her foot grasp vanishes between eight and fifteen months of age.

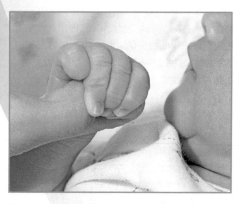

Placing your extended finger in your newborn's palm will cause her tiny fingers to grab your finger with amazing strength!

Place your thumb on the bottom of her foot under the toes and your baby's toes curl in.

Fencing Reflex

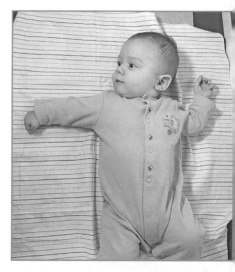

By four weeks of age, babies show another surprisingly cute reflex called the fencing reflex, also known as the asymmetrical tonic neck reflex. Simply turning your baby's head to the side will prompt the arm to extend, allowing her to sight along the extended arm to the outreached hand. What you are seeing is the first coordinated action between vision and reaching. How cute is that? By six months of age, this reflex disappears and your baby will proceed to bigger and better things.

Turn your baby's head to the side and watch his arm extend as he sights along the extended arm to his hand.

Startle Reflex

Have you ever noticed your baby flail his arms and cry when someone slams the door? This amazingly complex startle reflex, also called the Moro reflex, should reassure you because it means his nervous system is developing normally. A baby born before thirty-eight weeks gestation may not yet demonstrate the entire reflex, but by the time he meets his full-term age, this reflex should be evident. One way to prompt your baby's startle reflex is to raise his head a short distance while he is on his back. When his head is quickly lowered, his arms will fully extend. This is generally followed by his arms coming back towards his chest as your baby begins to cry. Is it any wonder we call it the startle reflex? This response gradually disappears by four months of age.

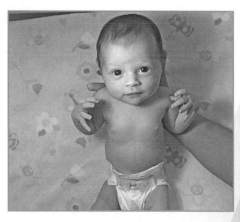

You can bring on your baby's startle reflex by raising her head slightly while she's on her back and then allow her head to quickly lower.

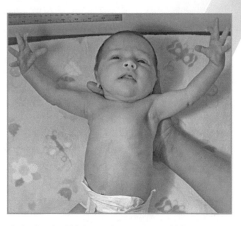

As her head quickly lowers, her arms extend fully.

Positive Support Reflex

Like the grasp reflex, this one is fun to demonstrate. Gently hold your baby around his chest and lower his feet until they touch a flat surface. At first, he may stand on his toes, but within thirty seconds, he will support himself on flat feet before gently sagging into a sitting position. For a brief moment, your baby's knees extended and he stood long enough to partially bear weight. By four months of age, this reflex will disappear and will be replaced by his ability to stand (when supported) and bounce for a much longer duration.

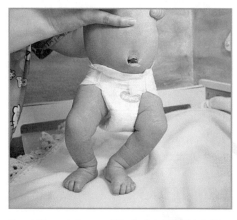

If you hold your baby around his chest and allow his feet to touch a flat surface, he stands on his toes. Then, within thirty seconds, he supports himself on flat feet.

Development by Age

Let's explore your baby's milestones, month by month.

One Month

At one month of age, your baby is no longer considered a newborn, but development is still dominated by a range of early reflexes. These reflexive responses set the stage for three broad areas of development that will evolve over time: Movement or motor skills; language; and social or interactive behaviors. While watching for your baby's changes, remember that development evolves over time. Stages do not necessarily present in any particular order and what may be evident one moment may not necessarily be repeated. Your baby will do what she wants when she wants or when she is ready to do it. One thing I can almost promise is that at the moment when you have an audience gathered to show off her new skills, she won't perform. Welcome to parenthood.

Motor Skills

When placed on his tummy, your baby will curl up into a tight ball with his arms drawn in and his knees tucked under his torso, occasionally turning his head from side to side. This comforting position is not much different than how he felt inside mom's womb. Although babies sleep comfortably in this position, it is important to always put them to bed on their back to reduce the chance of Sudden Infant Death Syndrome.

If your baby is placed on his tummy, he will curl up into a tight ball, like he was in mommy's tummy.

During his first month or two of age, your baby will exhibit amazing strength and lift his head up momentarily. If an object is held real close to his face, he may follow it momentarily, but only for a short distance.

Fist in mouth soothes a newborn.

Language

Language development in your baby involves both hearing and vocalizing. Long before her first words are uttered, your baby will respond to you and to environmental sounds. Playing soft music is a wonderful way to soothe your baby. During the first six weeks of life, your baby's eyes will widen and she will startle at loud sounds. She will also respond to your voice, sometimes by turning to a parent who is gently whispering. Early vocalization will start being evident during this period of time, although these very limited utterances pretty much consist of throaty noises and crying.

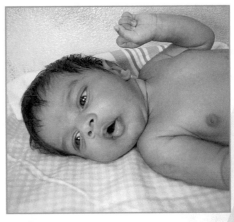

Notice the tightly clenched fist as this newborn tries to focus on his surroundings.

Social Behavior

We are fascinated by a newborn baby's face. Likewise, newborns are fascinated with our faces. Typically, babies can see for a range of eight to twelve inches (twenty to thirty centimeters). During the first month of life, they will occasionally focus on the person holding them. Such interactions may be brief because babies tend to turn away when they sense too much stimulation. By two months of age, a baby will return a smile.

Although your baby can see, and should be able to briefly track closely held objects that are moving slowly, his eye muscles are still very weak and may initially wander or appear cross-eyed. If, by three months of age, one eye still wanders independently of the other, or his eyes appear crossed, ask your physician to examine your baby's eyes.

Two Months

By two months of age, your baby will feel very comfortable with you. Although interaction is still limited, the attachment between you both should be strong and mutual. Her neck is getting stronger but she will still lack strength in her back. She will become more responsive and this shows through her wonderful array of sounds. There is nothing more endearing than your baby's smiles and coos!

By the time she is two months old, she begins relaxing from the tight bundle she once was when she rested on her tummy.

Motor Skills

When your baby reaches two months of age, he will begin relaxing from that tight bundle he used to be when he was placed on his tummy. You will notice how his hips are a little more extended and his shoulders are not pulled in so tight. If you place your baby on his back and gently pull both arms to raise him up to a sitting position, his head and shoulders should begin to rise with ease. His head will still lag behind his body when you pull both arms, but you should be able to see how his neck is getting much stronger. Likewise, if you prop him in a sitting position, his head starts to steady by four months of age.

If you place your baby on her back and gently pull both arms to raise her up to a sitting position, her head and shoulders should begin to rise with ease.

Between two and four months of age, your baby will be able to track a slowly moving object presented close to the face all the way from left to right. At about the same time he will start to bring his hands together and occasionally swipe at objects held closely in front of him. Placing a colorful mobile of varied shapes above his crib will provide hours of amusement for your baby.

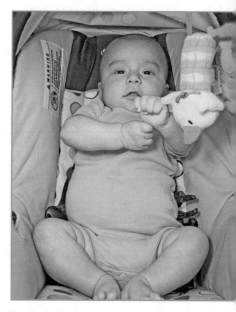

From two to four months of age, your baby occasionally swipes an object held closely in front of him.

Language

The sounds coming from your baby flourish by two months of age. You'll hear simple noises such as "ah," "ee," "coo," and "oh." These sounds, along with occasional grunts, gurgles and squeals, make wonderful music. An audible laugh can be heard between one and four months of age. You will know that your baby can hear because she may become quiet when you speak and may even blink when she hears other sounds. In addition, she will continue to turn toward voices that are soothing. If you like to sing, your baby will love to listen.

Social Behavior

Between one and three months of age there should be no mistaking that your baby can recognize you as his parent. He will calm down more easily to a familiar voice and smile to faces he knows. His smile will grow and become more spontaneous over the next few months as he starts noticing other people. Soon your baby will be lighting up a room with smiles.

Her smile grows and becomes more spontaneous over the next few months as she notices other people.

Three Months

Socially your baby is beaming with smiles and squeals. Now comes the time to master grasping objects. This is not an easy task when you consider that your baby still does not have enough strength to sit without support.

As his hands open more, he begins to suck on his thumbs and fingers.

His hands are no longer tightly fisted, showing that his grasp reflex has begun to fade.

Motor Skills

Notice how her hands are no longer tightly fisted. The grasp reflex has begun to fade. Early on, some babies enjoy sucking on their entire fist. Now that the hands are more open, infants begin to suck on their thumb or fingers. Your baby can grasp an object, although you may have to help your newborn by placing or releasing the object from his or her hand. Try introducing a rattle and see what your baby can do. This upper arm strength is also evident when your baby is placed on her tummy because, by three or four months of age, she will start to push up and lift her chest off the bed, supporting herself with the forearms.

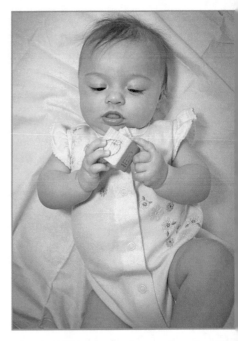

When handed to her, your newborn is able to grasp an object but you may have to help her by placing or releasing the object from her hand.

Language

I wish there was a button to turn on the squeals and raspberry noises that come from a baby between one and six months of age. When your baby feels talkative, these cute sounds fill a room and instantly grab everyone's attention.

Social Behavior

Smiling is still the primary source of social interaction. Babies instinctively know how to grab everyone's positive attention: **Just smile!** Watch as your baby smiles back when you smile. Try making other facial expressions and see how your baby responds. Each baby reacts differently but the connection is unmistakable. These moments are very special.

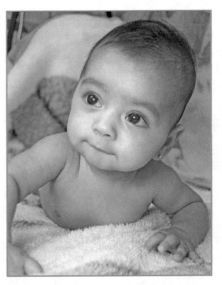

By the time she's three to four months of age, she will lift her chest from the surface, supporting herself with her arms.

Four Months

Now is the time to think about keeping your baby a good distance from small objects. To your baby, the world is meant to eat and the last thing you want is for your baby to choke on a small object. Child-friendly toys that are comfortable to grab and chew make play sessions worthwhile. Their improved strength and coordination make such interactions possible.

Motor Skills

Now that your baby has good neck control, you can prop him into a sitting position and have some fun. His back is still weak so he is likely to tumble often. Place a small object near your baby and watch as he uses his outstretched hand as a rake to pull that object closer to him. Between four and five months of age, your baby is able to bring small items towards him even though he has not figured out how best to use the fingers and thumb. Your baby will also have mastered grasping a rattle and, if given the chance, he will immediately begin to chew on it.

As strength continues to build in the upper body, your baby may attempt to roll over. Although many books will say babies roll from their tummy to their backs between three and five months of age, do not be surprised if it takes longer for your baby to reach this milestone. Now that babies are routinely placed on their backs during sleeping hours to reduce the chance of Sudden Infant Death Syndrome, this milestone is often not achieved so early. You should not be concerned and

Put a small object near him and watch as your baby's hand becomes a rake, pulling that object closer to him.

Your baby will roll from her back to her stomach by the time she's ten months old. She might do this even before she can roll from her stomach to her back.

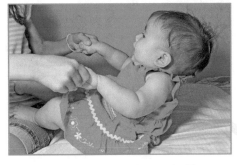

The head only lags slightly as your four-month-old is pulled to sitting.

this does not mean your baby requires more tummy time. Enjoy the movements of the moment. Your baby will be rolling along soon enough. Rolling from his back to his tummy will occur by ten months of age and may happen before he learns to roll from tummy to back.

Language

What a difference some neck control can make! Your baby can finally turn toward every imaginable noise. Her interest in sounds should reassure you that her hearing is well and vocalization will continue to progress. Babies learn by listening to others. Watch as she learns from the sounds around her. By handing her a baby-friendly musical toy, such as a bell or rattle, your baby will fill the room with music.

Social Behavior

Smiling is in full force by four months of age. Now that your sleepless nights are coming to an end, you should be smiling too. Have fun as your baby interacts and returns the smile of others. If you attach an unbreakable mirror to the inside of his crib, he will probably smile at himself all night.

Just when you thought your baby could sit by herself, she falls over again.

Five Months

Almost, almost, almost, plop! Just when you thought your baby could sit by herself, she falls over again. This will not stop your baby from grabbing everything in sight. Nor will it stop her from telling you of all of her accomplishments. You may not be able to understand what your baby is saying, but that little one is becoming quite the social butterfly.

Motor Skills

Babies will sit alone momentarily sometime between four and eight months of age. The back muscles are probably not strong enough yet for prolonged sitting, but your baby's strength has improved significantly. Remember a few months ago when you placed your newborn on his back and pulled both arms until he was raised in a sitting position? Try it again. Between four and six months of age your baby will be so strong that his head will pop right up without lagging behind the arms. You can tell that he is anticipating the pull of his arms. Somewhere between three and seven months of age, if you support him by the waist and lower the feet to the ground, your baby will stand and enjoy being gently bounced. This is fun for both you and your baby and will not harm the hips.

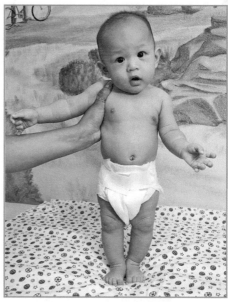

Somewhere between three and seven months of age, if you support him by the waist and lower the feet to the ground, your baby will stand and enjoy being gently bounced.

Look at his hands working too. Instead of simply grabbing objects, by five to seven months of age he will be able to transfer objects independently from one hand to the other. Textured toys that make sounds and objects that can be grasped with little fingers will amuse him for hours.

Your baby's back muscles are probably not strong enough for sitting. Still, he is getting stronger from four to eight months of age.

Language

The expressions on your baby's face become much more noticeable from this point forward. Between four and nine months of age, your baby will respond appropriately to happy voices and angry-sounding voices. Soon you will be able to reach for your baby, say "up," and expect raised arms in response. By four to eleven months of age, a wide array of babbling sounds will develop, many of which will arise without prompting. Soon you will hear sounds like "ba-ba-ba-ba" and other consonant-containing, nonspecific sounds that define babble.

Between five and seven months of age, your baby will start transferring objects from one hand to the other.

Social Behavior

In addition to that social smile that endures for so long, your baby is now set with the strength needed to have fun with her environment. Between four to ten months of age, a gentle game of tug-of-war is possible as your baby resists when you try pulling her favorite toy away. Remember to frequently check what is around your baby to avoid her accidental exposure to a choking hazard.

Her increased strength allows the head to pop right up when both hands are pulled.

Six Months

Your baby is now the master at getting the attention of others. Although he's not necessarily crawling yet, mobility is possible. Vocal interactions are possible too. The world is a fun place to explore and engage in, and your baby is in full control. Stand back and enjoy watching your baby take center stage.

Motor Skills

Between five and nine months of age, your baby will finally be able to sit without support, initially by leaning forward on her outstretched hands. Her head and back are now held straight and her ability to maintain a

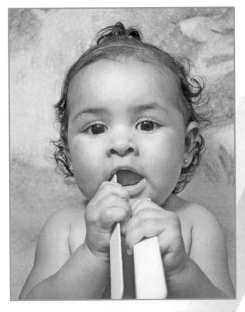

Now is the time for some serious interaction. When presented with two objects, do not be surprised if she takes one in each hand. The ability to operate each hand independently is gained between six and nine months of age.

sitting position is soon to follow. Now is the time for some serious interaction. When presented with two objects, do not be surprised if she takes one in each hand. The ability to operate each hand independently is gained between six and nine months. When placed on her tummy, early "commando" crawling may start. Babies will drag their legs and belly along the floor with those strong upper arms. Other children are content to sit and watch the world, showing little interest in moving from their location. Each baby is a unique person, with their own personality, and it's important to respect their individual needs, desires and achievements.

When placed on their bellies, babies will drag their legs and belly along the floor with their strong arms, "commando" style.

Language

If you have not noticed, your baby reliably responds to his name. They know who they are. A few months ago, your newborn may have vocalized the moment you spoke. Now your baby is likely to sit quietly and appear to "listen" to whoever is talking. The moment you stop talking they begin. When you speak they hush up. This back-and-forth "vocal tennis" can repeat many times and this is why bringing your baby to a movie theater or live performance can be very disruptive. The moment the room is quiet your baby will want to speak. All eyes are no longer on the stage. They are on your baby.

By seven to eleven months of age, babies learn to pick up small objects between their thumb and fingers.

Social Behavior

Between five and nine months of age, your baby is grabbing for everything out of reach. The more there is to touch, the happier he will be. Remember to fill his surroundings with toys of different textures and colors. Soft toys that make noise when rattled are perfect for this age. Let your little one explore baby books with cloth or vinyl pages. Learning to turn pages is a good way to introduce your baby to books.

From six to ten months of age, your baby will stand by holding onto you or another object.

From six to nine months of age, most babies are strong enough to push up on their hands and knees and crawl on all fours.

Seven Months to One Year

If your baby is not sitting yet, that milestone is soon to follow. Mobility is also likely to progress, although the pace will vary depending on what your baby wishes to accomplish. If the immediate environment is sufficiently entertaining, why bother moving far? The ability to grasp objects and make impressive sounds is stimulation enough for many babies this age.

Motor Skills

Between six and nine months of age, babies are strong enough to push themselves up on their hands and knees and creep on all four extremities. For many, this form of transportation serves them well. By seven to eleven months of age, babies who are lying down will also sit by themselves. If placed in a standing position at six to ten months of age, your baby will stand by holding onto you. Standing alone comes between nine and sixteen months of age. By the time your baby is a year old, she should be able to pull herself to a stand and cruise around while holding onto furniture. Actual walking may not occur until fifteen months of age.

Her hands are becoming useful tools. By seven to thirteen months of age, objects she holds in each hand will be banged together. The fingers also come into play as babies, by seven to eleven months of age, learn to pick up small objects between their thumb and finger. The ability to be precise might not come until fourteen months of age. Watch

In one short year, your baby evolves from a seemingly simple array of newborn reflexes to a playful, interactive bundle of joy.

your baby master stacking toys of different colors, shapes and sizes. Everything becomes a toy at this age: dolls, trucks, puppets, push-pull toys, and even egg cartons, large plastic bottles and empty boxes. Let the exploration begin!

Language

What could be more fun for a baby than imitating words that are spoken by others? By six to eleven months of age, that is what your baby will be doing. At ten months of age, you may even hear what sounds like the word "mama" or "dada." That "mama" and "dada" sound will be spoken with purpose by fourteen months of age as your baby makes clear that he knows who you are when he says "mama" and "dada." The next understandable word might not be heard until sixteen months of age. We have been led to believe that speech flourishes at the first birthday. I remind parents that their understanding of what you say increases after they turn a year, but what they say is often limited until after they turn two. Have fun reading to your baby and letting him negotiate baby-friendly books. His comprehension will amaze you.

Have fun reading to your baby and letting her negotiate baby-friendly books. Her comprehension will amaze you.

Social Behavior

Social behavior flourishes over this period of time. That smile, offered to anybody who would pay attention to him, is now reserved for those special people in your baby's life. It's also that special attachment which allows your voice to soothe your baby when crying. Likewise, when you walk out of your baby's sight, don't be surprised if she begins crying. A familiar person is comforting to your baby, while unfamiliar people may cause a baby to squirm and cry. The extent of their reactions will vary depending on your baby's temperament. Some babies are comfortable around strangers, while others quickly shy away. When there is a special attachment established between you and your baby, her ability to indicate her desires without crying is facilitated. This skill is usually achieved between eleven and fifteen months of age.

Fun games like peek-a-boo can be played between six and ten months of age. Pat-a-cake soon follows between seven and thirteen months of age. Playing peek-a-boo is a milestone marked by your baby's new awareness of object permanence. Before your baby is six months old, take her favorite toy and completely cover it with a blanket. Chances are she will make no effort to uncover the toy. At some point after, when you once again hide her toy, your baby will actively reach under the blanket to find her toy. Your baby remembers that she has a toy and where it is. Similarly, when your baby covers her eyes, she remembers you are still present. Object permanence has been achieved.

In one short year your baby's skills evolved from a seemingly simple array of newborn reflexes to a playful and interactive bundle of joy. Her personality and temperament are what makes your baby unique. Hold onto those early moments as she grows. Seeing these qualities in your older child is what makes her your baby for life.

Everything is fun now that your baby is strong enough to explore the world.

Notes

Chapter 2

Rashes, Rashes, Rashes

Newborn Rashes Explained.

For all the talk about the beauty of newborn skin, I am always amazed at how many harmless rashes a newborn develops. Fortunately, your baby will probably only display a couple of these skin markings and most will resolve in short order. Some are so common and fleeting, your baby's doctor may not even mention them. Before you start searching the Internet and scaring yourself, let us discuss the common rashes. Knowing what you see should ease your concerns.

● ●

Salmon Patch

These blood vessel clusters are seen on more than half of all newborns and have a host of fun names. On the back of the neck, just under the hairline, this mark is called a stork bite (as if a stork had carried your baby). If seen on the forehead, on the upper eyelid or above the nose, it is referred to as an angel kiss. In addition they may be found on your baby's lower back. Salmon patches appear as a pinkish flame-shaped patch that blanches when one gently applies pressure with their thumb. Most fade within the first year of life, although the stork bite and patch on the lower back may persist indefinitely. Watch when your baby cries and you will see this patch become more intense in color. It looks serious, but it's really harmless. Fortunately, the facial patches almost always disappear as your baby matures.

Salmon Patches: A pink, flame-shaped patch that turns white when gently pressed.

Salmon Patch cont.

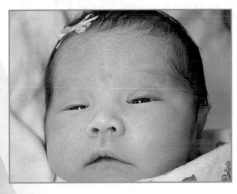

Angel Kisses: Found on the forehead, upper eyelids or above the nose.

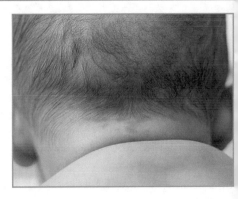

Stork Bite: On the back of the neck, just under the hairline.

Acne

The hormones running through your newborn can cause acne within the first two to three weeks of life. This mimics adult acne, with the face and upper chest being affected. Unlike adult acne, no treatment is necessary. This condition usually resolves in a month or two, although it may persist longer.

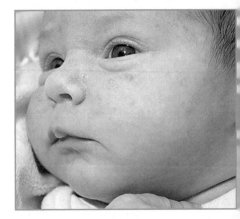

Baby Acne: Mimics adult acne, with the face and upper chest being affected.

Heat Rash

Also known as prickly heat or miliaria rubra in Latin, this scattered rash will appear on the face, neck and upper torso of any infant during periods of warm, humid weather. Dressing your newborn loosely or moving your infant to a cooler location will help speed the clearing of this harmless rash.

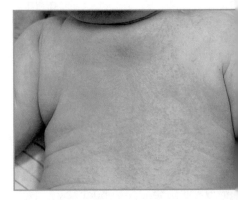

Heat Rash: Can appear on an infant's face, neck and upper torso when the weather is hot and humid.

Sucking Blister

The sucking reflex is so powerful that newborns will latch onto just about anything. I was convinced that my little girl would have latched onto a light switch if I let her. Before they get out in the world and latch onto you, they will suck on themselves. The upper lip and hand are common areas where sucking blisters are evident. Within six months of age, these marks will disappear.

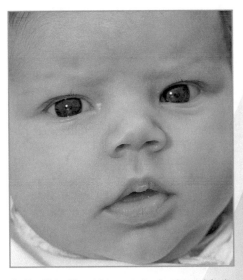

Sucking Blister: These blisters are often found on an infant's upper lip or hand.

Milia

Unlike the white dots commonly seen on the nose of newborns, milia are small cysts that develop from hair follicles. These harmless whitish-yellow cysts, often seen below the eyes, require no treatment and usually disappear on their own within the first few years of your baby's life.

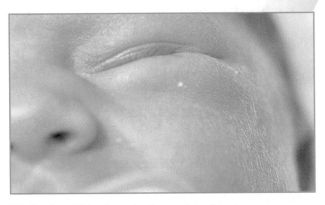

Milia: Harmless whitish-yellow cysts, often seen below the eyes.

Sebaceous Glands

Small white bumps cover the nose of many newborns. These tiny bumps disappear within four to six months and do not require treatment.

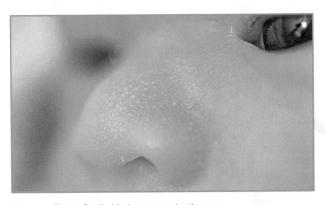

Sebaceous Glands: Small white bumps covering the nose.

Mottled

Also known in Latin as cutis marmorata, mottling is seen in nearly all newborns. This bluish-purple netlike discoloration of the skin is most evident when your newborn is cool and disappears as your baby warms up. By six months of age, most babies are big enough for mottling not to occur. Although harmless and seen in all children, in the rare instance that mottling is always present and prominent, it is important to talk with your doctor and be assured that this is normal.

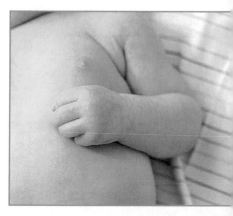

Mottled: This bluish-purple netlike discoloration of the skin mostly appears when your newborn is cool and disappears a your baby warms up.

Erythema Toxicum Neonatorum

Although the name may sound scary, this common rash is very harmless. Often mistaken for flea bites, erythema toxicum is easy to identify by its blotchy red base and central, pinpoint whitish-yellow bump. It appears within the first two to four days after your baby's birth and fully resolves by the second or third week of life. Nearly half of all newborns will develop this rash, which most commonly appears on the chest, back, face, and both the upper arms and legs. What's funny about this rash is that the baby's palms and soles are spared.

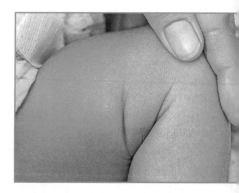

Erythema Toxicum Neonatorum: Easy to identify by its blotchy red base and central, pinpoint whitish-yellow bump.

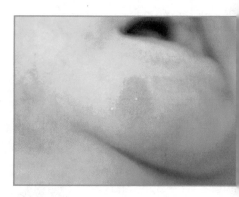

Erythema Toxicum Neonatorum

Peeling

A newborn born close to his or her due date should have moist, smooth skin at first. But within the next day or two after birth, it is common for peeling to occur. This process may take three weeks to resolve. Once the peeling finishes, the underlying skin should again be normal in appearance. Applying lotion is not necessary but if you really want to, apply perfume-free baby lotion to the dry patches. Do not apply lotion to your baby's face.

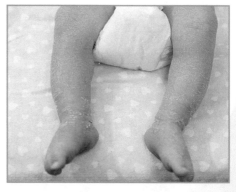

Peeling: Once the peeling finishes, the underlying skin should look normal.

Mongolian Spot

Often mistaken for a bruise, Mongolian spots are irregular-shaped bluish-black patches of extra pigment. Although they most commonly show up on your baby's lower back and buttocks, they can be found on any skin surface. Mongolian spots occur in all races but are most evident on dark-skinned babies. Most spots gradually disappear on their own by the time your baby is five years old.

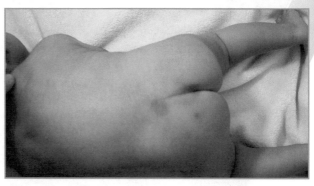

Mongolian Spots: Irregular-shaped bluish-black patches of extra pigment.

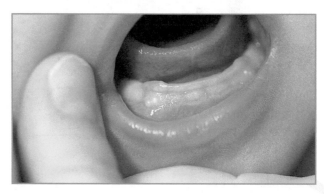

Gum Cysts: Whitish cysts are harmless and resolve by themselves within a few weeks.

Gum Cysts

Sometimes cysts will form on the gums of your baby's mouth. These whitish cysts are harmless and resolve on their own within a few weeks.

Epstein Pearl

If you open your baby's mouth and look closely at the roof, you may notice one or more white cysts. These are called Epstein pearls and, like the gum cysts, they are harmless and fade away within a few weeks.

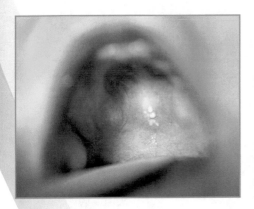

Epstein Pearl

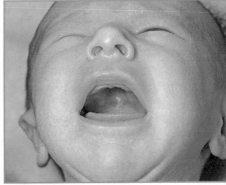

Epstein Pearl: One or more white cysts that appear on the roof of a baby's mouth.

Skin Tags

Development can often lead to funny findings. Skin tags fall into this category. These harmless skin appendages can sometimes be seen just in front of the ear. Rarely, more than one will form. For those who find such tags to be distasteful, ask your baby's physician about having the skin tag removed. This can often be done during the first few weeks of life.

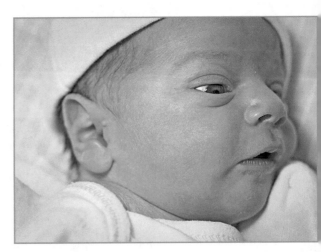

Skin Tags: These harmless skin appendages are sometimes found just in front of the ear.

Conjunctival Hemorrhage

f delivery was difficult, chances are your baby became a little bruised in the process of entering this world. Occasionally the force is so great that a blood vessel in the white of the eye will break. This will result in a crescent-shaped red streak adjacent to the eyeball. No need to worry. The vision will not be affected and within a few weeks this small hemorrhage will resolve.

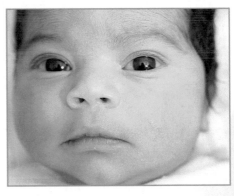

Conjunctival Hemorrhage: A broken blood vessel in the white of the eye.

Hemangioma

Within your infant's first month or two of life, you might find a soft, spongy, bright red region of skin. Although hemangiomas are rarely visible at birth, they can grow rapidly during that first year of your baby's life and then slowly disappear by the time your child turns nine years old. Their size and location may vary and although most fade away, some may become a permanent mark on your child. Although most are harmless and require no treatment, a physician should periodically confirm that their size and location do not pose a problem for your baby. This is especially true for midline hemangiomas or those near the eyes, airway, anus or genital region.

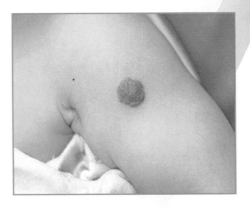

Hemangioma: A soft, spongy, bright red region of skin.

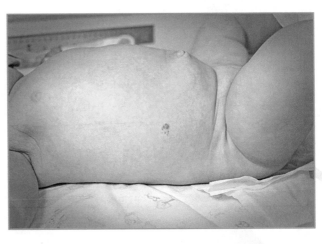

Hemangioma: These rapidly growing lesions are rarely visible at birth.

Notes

Chapter 3

Baby Care that Nobody Talks About

Common Baby Issues Explained.

This chapter is why you will probably not keep this book around on the coffee table for others to see. It's too bad because some topics deserve both an explanation and a picture. Try not to cringe and let us discuss a few items that are commonly asked by parents like you.

• •

Bundling

I have a secret. When I see a crying baby for the first time, I bundle him snugly, rock him gently, and peek at his parents as they wonder how I calmed their baby so quickly. Truthfully, this secret technique has been used for ages. Many authors have tried to adopt this technique as their own, but bundling is universally known and it is a skill well worth your time to master.

The key to successful bundling is start with a taut blanket that has little stretch. Cotton flannel blankets are ideal for calming babies because the cotton flannel is soft and comfortable, yet babies cannot easily wiggle free once snugly bundled.

Begin by laying the blanket flat. Fold one corner over a few inches and lay your baby face-up on the blanket. His shoulders should be just below the fold. Wrap one side of the blanket over your baby and snugly tuck it under him. Do not be timid. You want your baby to be tightly wrapped. When bundling, both his arms should be fully extended at your baby's side and tucked under the blanket. Fold the bottom corner up and over his feet. Finally, wrap the other side of the blanket around your baby.

Once wrapped, some babies will continue to squirm for a couple of minutes. Gently rock him for a few minutes and, more often than not, your baby will calm. Newborns are comfortable when bundled snugly and can be swaddled for up to twenty hours each day. It is very unlikely that you will wrap your baby too tight. If you can slide your hand gently between the blanket and your baby's chest, it is not too tight.

When bundled, your baby should be slightly warm to touch and not sweaty. A sweaty baby, who is hot and red, is overwrapped and might also be wearing too many clothes. When deciding how many layers of clothing to put on your baby, think about how many layers you need to remain warm and then add one layer. If you require one layer of clothing to stay warm in your home, a baby will require two layers, typically pajamas and a bundling blanket.

By four months of age, bundling becomes unnecessary and potentially dangerous. When babies learn to wiggle out of their bundle, the loose blanket can wrap around a baby's face. This is why a loose blanket should never be left in bed with your baby. Be certain to remove all loose objects from your baby's bed area when he is sleeping.

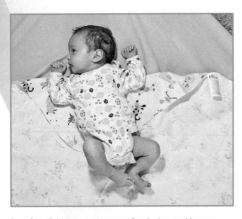

Step One: Fold one corner over a few inches and lay your baby face-up on the blanket.

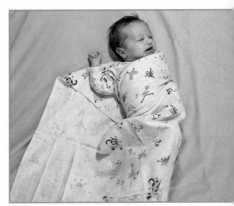

Step Two: Wrap one side of the blanket over your baby and snugly tuck it under him.

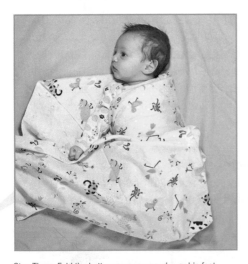

Step Three: Fold the bottom corner up and over his feet.

Step Four: Finally, wrap the other side of the blanket around your baby.

Umbilical Cord Care

The appearance of this little rubbery, wet stump can cause many people to cringe. Yet the umbilical cord served a key role in providing the blood supply from the placenta to your baby. Now that the cord has been clipped, you need to wait patiently for it to dry out and fall off. Typically this takes one to three weeks.

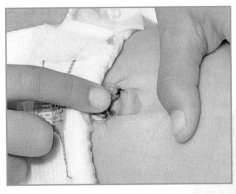

Don't be scared to pull the cord back and clean its base. Otherwise it can start to smell really bad.

Caring for the umbilical cord until it falls off is simple. Some parents choose to do nothing. With time it will fall off on its own. I prefer to pull the cord back and clean the base with a cotton ball or cotton swab dipped in either water or rubbing alcohol. I clean the base because otherwise it will begin to smell really bad. When the cord has dried out sufficiently it will eventually pull right off with a gentle tug. This is safe to do and will not harm your baby.

Once the umbilical cord comes off, do not be surprised to see a few drops of fresh blood and possibly some clear secretions where the cord fell off. Remember, this was the place handling the blood supply for your baby and some trapped blood is still in the cord. Within a few days the area where the cord fell off will begin to dry out, leaving a normal-appearing belly button.

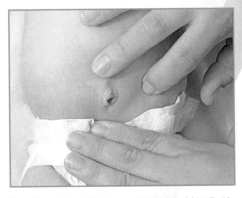

When the cord does fall off, some dried blood might collect in the belly button.

Although infection around the umbilical cord or belly button is rare, intense redness and/or pus around the umbilical cord must be shown to a physician immediately. Also, call your baby's doctor if the umbilical cord does not fall off within three weeks.

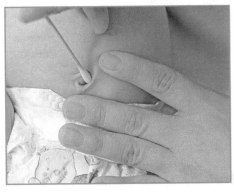

Clean the base of the umbilical cord with a cotton ball or cotton swab dipped in either water or rubbing alcohol.

Newborn Vaginal Discharge

The mother's hormones circulating throughout your newborn girl may cause your baby to develop a clear or white vaginal discharge. Also, the genital region may seem quite large and puffy. This is normal and any discharge may be gently cleaned with a mild soap and water by washing the genital region from front to back.

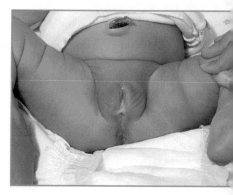

The mother's hormones circulating throughout your newborn girl may cause your baby to develop a clear or white vaginal discharge.

Circumcision

Circumcision involves removing the foreskin, a small piece of skin from the end of a boy's penis. Most physicians perform this procedure within the first few days of life. Although a circumcised male is less likely to develop a urinary tract infection, the risk is not significant enough to guide your decision. This is a personal choice. There really is no right or wrong answer.

If you choose not to have your child circumcised, caring for your baby boy's penis is very simple. During the first year of life, use a mild soap and water to wash the external genitalia. As long as your boy has a good stream of urine when he urinates, gentle cleaning is all your newborn requires. Your physician will talk to you about when the foreskin should be pulled back to expose the head of the penis. Usually, this will be after your son turns three years old, because the adhesions preventing the foreskin from being pulled back begin to loosen at this age.

If your newborn will be circumcised, it helps to know how a normally healing penis will look. The skin will appear pink and some yellow crusting may be evident. Your baby's physician may wrap the penis in gauze or recommend that an ointment be applied. Often, all that is required is some petroleum jelly (Vaseline®) on the wound site for a few days to prevent the penis from sticking to the diaper. You may gently clean the surrounding skin, but there is no need to clean the healing penis. Within a week, the circumcision should be healed.

Call your physician immediately if your baby's penis develops signs of infection, such as a thick green discharge, redness, swelling, or if a red streak develops on the shaft of the penis. If the site bleeds to the point where the blood starts to puddle, call immediately for emergency help and further instructions. Other warning signs in your baby that require prompt medical attention include fever, fussiness, irritability, no urine within twelve hours, a high-pitched cry, no desire to eat, or if the circumcision site does not heal within one week. If your physician uses a device called a Plastibell®, which is a clear plastic ring left on the penis after a circumcision, call your baby's physician if the Plastibell® does not fall off after ten days.

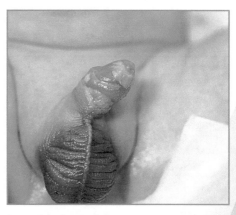

A normally healing circumcised penis on a newborn will look pink and some yellow crusting may be present.

Adhesion After Circumcision

During the first few months of your baby boy's life after he's been circumcised, the head of his penis may reattach at its base to the shaft of the penis where the circumcision was performed. If reattachment of this skin occurs, speak with your baby's physician about how to gently separate the adhesion. Once this attachment is separated, you should gently pull the skin back each time your baby is bathed to help prevent reattachment.

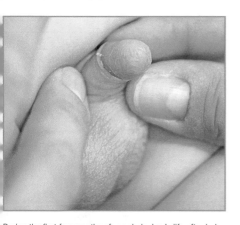

During the first few months of your baby boy's life after he's been circumcised, the head of his penis may reattach at its base to the shaft of the penis where the circumcision was performed.

If reattachment of this skin occurs, speak with your baby's physician about how to gently separate the adhesion.

Notes

Chapter 4

Those Messy Diapers

Is This Normal?

Concerns about baby poop are common among parents. But, there is rarely a need to be worried. If the stool comes out hard as a rock or white as a ghost, speak with your baby's physician. Otherwise things are probably normal. Let's take a look at just what is normal in the poop department.

Newborns poop a lot. That's why diaper companies stay in business! A natural reflex prompts babies to fill their diaper shortly after feeding. With an average of eight feedings a day, things can pile up very quickly. Despite these averages, normal stool frequency can vary considerably. A baby may poop seven times per day or once every seven days. If the tummy remains soft and the baby is not throwing up, all is probably normal. Infrequent stooling does not mean your baby is constipated. Hard, pellet-like poops define constipation.

Another concern among parents is how loose the stools look. Baby stool, especially among breast-fed infants, is very runny. Diarrhea in newborns is rare. If you are still concerned that your baby has diarrhea, watch her weight. During the first week of life, your baby will lose up to eight percent of her birth weight. For a baby weighing eight pounds (3.6 kilograms) this is about ten ounces (280 grams). By two weeks of life, your baby should be back to her birth weight. If your newborn has not regained her birth weight by two weeks of age, talk to your baby's doctor about the possible causes. It's probably not because of diarrhea. Most likely your baby is not taking in enough breast milk or formula.

One last point to keep in mind: At six weeks of age your baby will likely poop less frequently. Mark your calendar and watch. Your newborn will probably go from multiple stools per day to once every few days. I can't explain why this happens, but I do know that babies tend to get fussier when this occurs and they also cry for longer periods of time. Colic, starting on page 68, will give you some ideas on how best to manage this situation.

• •

Meconium

How it is that a sweet and adorable newborn is able to expel something so sticky and tarry is beyond me! But they do and we are left to clean it up. Meconium is a thick, nearly black substance that has sat in the intestine for quite some time. Fortunately it is fairly odorless. Within a couple of days this will be out of your baby and the stools will begin to turn a yellow-green color.

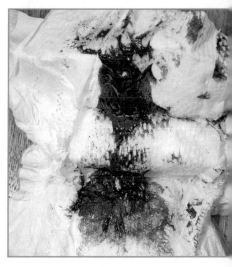

Meconium is a thick, nearly black substance that has sat in the intestine for quite some time.

Bottle-fed Diaper

When a baby is formula-fed, his stools often appear a little more firm and slightly darker than those of breast-fed infants. Also, formula-fed babies tend to poop less frequently than infants fed by breast milk. This is not constipation and this is not due to the iron added to the formula. This is normal.

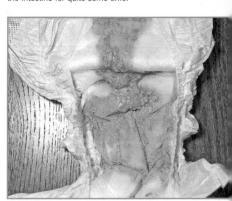

If a baby is formula-fed, the stools look firmer and darker than those of a breast-fed baby.

Breast-fed Diaper

If you are breast-feeding your baby, expect frequent stools that have the consistency of pea soup. These yellow stools have a very mild odor and can appear very loose.

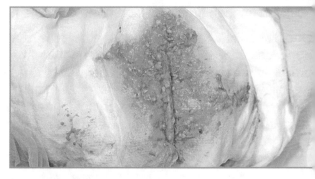

The stool of a breast-fed baby will be yellowish, have the consistency of pea soup, have a mild odor and can look very loose.

Urate Crystals

Often mistaken for blood, urate crystals are a normal, common occurrence and something you should be able to identify. When the urine becomes very concentrated, a pinkish stain may appear on the inside of the diaper towards the front. This is not blood. This brick-red color is formed by urate crystals that precipitate out of the urine when the urine is very concentrated. As

It's easy to mistake urate crystals for blood, but this common occurrence is something you should be able to identify.

your baby eats more, the urine will become less concentrated, more wet diapers will be produced, and the urate crystals should disappear. If, by day four of life, your baby is still producing this pinkish stain, speak with your baby's doctor. It is time for a weight check to ensure that your baby is being sufficiently fed.

Notes

Notes

Chapter 5

Minor Medical Problems

Simple Solutions to Common Problems.

It's time to put your doctor hat on. Here is a peek at a handful of common problems that have simple solutions. Put away grandma's secret home remedies. The correct treatments at the onset will save you much aggravation and perhaps an insurance co-pay or two.

● ●

Diaper Rashes

Parents pride themselves on having a rash-free child. When a diaper rash does develop, we mark this as a personal failure. Truthfully, no one is to blame. The most diligent parent will eventually be battling their child's diaper rash. It's not your fault. Let's talk about prevention and how to deal with the inevitable.

Newborn skin is very delicate. Protecting the skin is the key to success. Applying a protective ointment on all surfaces and creases of the diaper region after EVERY diaper change is a simple way to keep your baby rash-free. Should your baby have a wet or soiled diaper, this added barrier will help protect the skin.

Newborn skin is very delicate. Protecting the skin is the key to success and a happy baby.

Choose a diaper ointment that is not greasy and easy to apply. The goal is simply to add a protective barrier. Do not worry about zinc oxide and other healing agents. These ingredients have their place, but are unnecessary on healthy skin.

Next comes frequent diaper changes. It is the messy, poopy diaper that sets the stage for diaper rashes. The sooner poopy diapers are removed and disposed of, the better. For newborns, expect to change the diaper every few hours during the day and at least once each night. Super-absorbent disposable diapers are very effective, although cloth diapers that are not fitted too tight will work too. Diaper wipes are fine to use, but do not scrub or you will irritate the skin. Save the wiping for those poopy moments and simply change the diaper without wiping when it is wet. Surprisingly, urine against the skin is harmless and more damage can be done by wiping vigorously than merely changing a wet diaper without wiping. Do not forget to apply some more diaper rash ointment. The added barrier is essential.

Avoid using powders on your baby's bottom. Although powder traps moisture, it does not act as a barrier. Whatever gets absorbed by the powder still has contact with the skin. Also, when dressing your baby, never place plastic pants over a diaper. The plastic will trap moisture, could cause her skin to be damaged, and lead to a diaper rash.

These three simple steps will help prevent most diaper rashes:

1. Change diapers frequently with ultra-absorbent diapers.

2. Wipe but do not scrub the skin when changing a soiled mess.

3. Apply a diaper rash cream after every diaper change.

This approach will keep most newborns rash-free. Despite our best efforts, rashes can still happen, and there are several different types of rashes. A few pictures of different types of diaper rashes will quickly make you a treatment expert.

Irritant Contact Diaper Dermatitis

Think common, common, common. This simple diaper rash is easy to spot and, if treated quickly, will resolve with ease. The first areas I look at when trying to understand the cause of a diaper rash are the crease or skin folds of the baby's diaper region. Are the creases rash-free or red? If the creases are spared but the bottom and other large surfaces of the diaper region are red, this is probably irritant contact dermatitis. What do I mean by this?

This common diaper rash is easy to identify and can be simply resolved if treated quickly.

First, let us review some basic medical terminology. "Derm" is Greek for skin and "itis" means inflammation. So dermatitis is just a fancy word for inflammation of the skin. Any diaper rash is dermatitis. The skin is inflamed.

So what is the most common cause of irritant dermatitis? A soiled diaper. Stool is far more irritating than urine. That is why frequent diaper changes and a protective layer of a diaper rash ointment are essential.

Once the skin barrier is damaged, the skin will become red and slightly swollen. In typical irritant contact dermatitis, the creases in the groin area should be normal and rash-free. If left untreated, eventually even the creases will become red. Simple steps will help to quickly resolve this rash.

Frequent diaper changes are essential. When changing your baby's diaper, do not scrub his skin. Although diaper wipes may be used, they can sting the skin when a rash is present. If the diaper is only wet, do not wipe. When soiled, gentle cleaning with a mild soap in warm water is all you need to do.

Once his skin is clean, apply a thick diaper rash ointment. Now is the time to use an ointment with zinc oxide. This will soothe his skin and make it heal faster. If the skin is very red, you may wish to apply a thin layer of hydrocortisone cream 0.5% BEFORE applying the diaper rash ointment. If the barrier is applied first, the hydrocortisone can't work because it can't reach the skin.

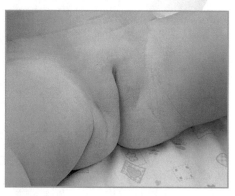

This simple method of combining frequent diaper changes, a barrier cream, and perhaps a little hydrocortisone cream 0.5% will resolve most causes of irritant contact dermatitis within a few days. Any rash that gets worse despite these simple steps must be evaluated by your baby's physician.

The first areas I look at when trying to understand the cause of a diaper rash are the skin folds of the baby's diaper region.

WARNING:

Unless directed otherwise by your baby's physician, only use the hydrocortisone cream 0.5% once daily for three days at most. Long-term use of hydrocortisone will damage the skin.

Candidal Diaper Dermatitis

A type of yeast called Candidal albicans is a common cause of diaper rashes. Usually, irritant contact dermatitis develops first. Once the baby's skin is damaged, yeast invades.

Yeast is everywhere in our environment and it likes to grow in moist, warm areas. When your baby's skin is damaged, yeast will invade and grow. Spotting this infection is important for selecting the right treatment.

Unlike simple irritant contact dermatitis, yeast likes to settle in the skin folds. The skin in the baby's diaper region often becomes very red. In addition, small beefy red spots with a donut-shaped white ring around them will develop on the surface of your baby's bottom. This rash may spread to the front and can even extend up towards your baby's belly.

Once yeast is present, treatment becomes more difficult. This is because the skin needs to heal and yeast likes to spread.

First, check to see how far the yeast has spread. It is amazing where yeast will grow. Check your baby's mouth. Has thrush developed? A glance at a photograph of thrush on page 49 will help you identify this common problem. If thrush is present, your baby's physician will assist in treatment. Also check all of the skin folds on your baby's body. This includes the neck, behind the ears, the armpits, and

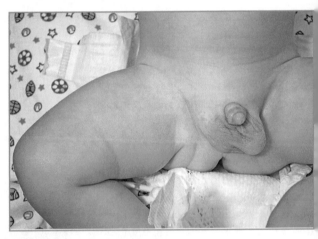

A type of yeast called Candidal albicans is a common cause of diaper rashes. Usually, irritant contact dermatitis develops first. Once the baby's skin is damaged, yeast invades, especially in the skin folds.

between the fingers and toes. If these areas are pink and greasy, they must also be treated.

Next, it is time to eliminate the yeast. An antifungal cream such as clotrimazole cream 1% or miconazole nitrate cream 2% can be purchased at any pharmacy. Apply twice daily for about four weeks. You should continue treatment for at least one week after the rash has finally resolved. Be sure to cover all pink rashes, including the neck and other skin folds, if a rash is present.

Finally, it is important to also treat the underlying irritant contact dermatitis that

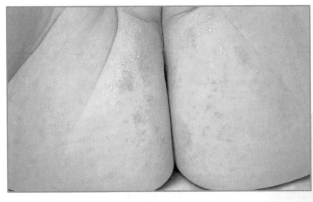

caused the skin to break down. Apply a diaper rash ointment with zinc oxide over the clotrimazole cream 1% or miconazole cream 2% and be sure to cover the entire diaper region. Never apply the barrier cream first or the antifungal cream will not be able to reach the skin.

Yeast is everywhere in our environment and it likes to grow in moist, warm areas. Notice the white donut-shaped rings that develop when yeast is present.

This simple method of applying antifungal cream on the infection followed by a barrier cream, and then coupled with frequent diaper changes, should have your baby's skin healed in two to four weeks. If the rash is getting worse despite your efforts, it is time for a visit to your baby's doctor.

HINT: If the skin is very red, mix a little pea-sized amount of hydrocortisone cream 0.5% with the clotrimazole cream 1% or miconazole nitrate cream 2%, but only use hydrocortisone once daily for three days at most to avoid damaging the skin. After three days, continue with the antifungal cream and diaper rash ointment with zinc oxide until the infection is resolved. Expect complete healing within four weeks. Diaper rashes that do not resolve within four weeks or that get worse despite treatment require medical attention.

Bacterial Diaper Dermatitis

As with yeast, bacteria are everywhere. When the skin is damaged, bacteria may invade and start to grow. Without proper treatment, this infection can spread rapidly. Evaluation by your baby's physician is essential.

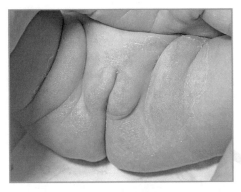

The presence of pus-filled pimples on a red base is the first clue that bacteria are present. Crusted lesions may also appear. If the skin is raw, blisters form, or if your baby appears ill or develops a fever, immediate medical attention is necessary. Unfortunately, over-the-counter remedies will not clear this kind of infection.

When the skin is damaged, bacteria may invade and start growing. Without proper treatment, this infection can spread rapidly. Evaluation by your baby's physician is essential.

Seborrhea

It is time to take a close look at your baby. Look behind the ears. Now gently lift the chin and check the neck. Do not forget your baby's armpits or the creases in the groin. If any of these areas have a pink or salmon-colored, greasy rash, think seborrhea.

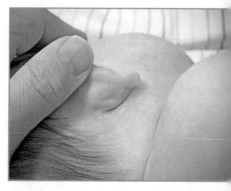

Look behind the ears. If this area has a pink or salmon-colored, greasy rash, think seborrhea.

Now check the scalp. Are there yellow-crusted flakes on the hair? This is another form of seborrhea that we call cradle cap. Sometimes a baby's eyebrows will become yellow crusted too.

Seborrhea is at its worst between four weeks and four months of life, but it may persist up to one year or longer. The cause is unknown and treatments vary. Here is one approach.

Should your baby have cradle cap, baby shampoo and a scrub brush should do the trick. Gently scrub until the yellow crusting is gone. Should the crusting reappear (and it probably will), just scrub it off again. Persistence is the key until your baby outgrows this condition.

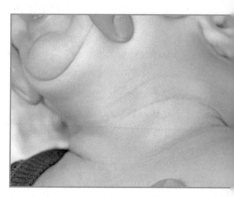

Gently lift the chin and check the neck. If you see a pink or salmon-colored, greasy rash, think seborrhea.

If your baby's skin folds become pink and greasy, treatment is a bit different. Many of these pink patches have become infected with yeast. The treatment is two-fold because you must reduce the inflammation and also eliminate the yeast.

First, apply an over-the-counter antifungal cream to the rash twice daily for a few weeks. Clotrimazole cream 1% or miconazole nitrate cream 2% are appropriate antifungal creams to use and they should be continued until at least one week has passed without signs

Cradle cap is another form of seborrhea that causes yellow-crusted flakes on the scalp.

of seborrhea. If resolution takes longer than four weeks, your baby must be evaluated by a physician.

The second step involves reducing inflammation. Simply mix a pea-sized amount of hydrocortisone cream 0.5% to the antifungal cream once daily for a maximum of three days. After three days, be sure to stop the hydrocortisone cream or damage to the skin may result.

Seborrhea should clear quickly. A physician should evaluate any rash that persists. If at any time your baby's skin begins to peel, appears beefy red, or if your baby is ill or has a fever, seek medical attention immediately.

Thrush

Thrush is yeast that grows in the mouth. Yeast likes warm, moist places to grow. The mouth is an ideal environment. Cheesy-white patches may be evident on your baby's lips, tongue or inside the mouth along the walls of his cheeks.

Sometimes breast milk or formula will coat the baby's tongue and look like thrush, but you should be able to easily wipe this off. Thrush is hard to remove with scraping. When thrush is present,

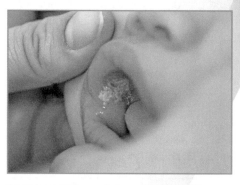

Thrush is yeast that grows in the mouth. Cheesy-white patches may be evident on your baby's lips, tongue or inside the mouth along the walls of his cheeks.

your baby's doctor will prescribe an oral medicine to eliminate this mild problem. If you're breast-feeding, speak with your physician about using an antifungal cream on your breasts to eliminate yeast.

When thrush is present, be sure to look for a Candidal diaper rash on your baby as discussed on page 46. The same yeast that causes thrush can also grow in the crease of the diaper region. If all signs of yeast are not treated, thrush will likely keep coming back.

Blocked Tear Duct

Tears prevent our eyes from drying out. They run across our eyes and drain into the nose through a small tube at the inside corner of the eye. In babies, this tube or tear duct can easily become blocked.

When the tear ducts are blocked, your baby's eyes will look very watery. White discharge may also form at the inside corner of her eye(s). After long naps, your baby's eyelashes will become sticky. Cleaning is simple: Use a cotton ball dipped

Blocked Tear Duct cont.

in sterile water; it is ideal for wiping the eyelid. Always wipe from the corner of her nose out and use a fresh cotton ball with each wipe.

If the white of the eye should become red, an infection has probably occurred and your baby must be evaluated by a physician. Sometimes the discharge in the corner of the eye will become thick and green. Your baby's doctor should also look at this because an antibiotic eye drop may be necessary. By six to twelve months of life, most tear ducts will fully open. Should they remain blocked past one year of age, your baby's physician will discuss treatment options.

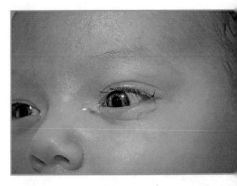

When the tear ducts are blocked, your baby's eyes will look very watery. White discharge may also form at the inside corner of her eye.

Umbilical Granuloma

Once the umbilical cord falls off, a little bit of the cord may remain. This is called an umbilical granuloma. If this piece of moist umbilical cord does not dry out within a month of life, your baby's doctor may apply a drying medication called silver nitrate. Within one week, that piece of umbilical cord should be gone.

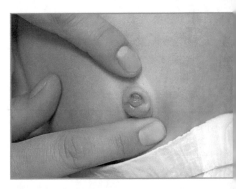

Once the umbilical cord falls off, a little bit of the cord may remain. This is called an umbilical granuloma.

Umbilical Hernia

The muscles on your baby's stomach are very weak. When a bulge forms by the belly button, this is called an umbilical hernia. By three years of age, the muscles will become stronger and the hernia should disappear. Straps that push the hernia in are unnecessary and

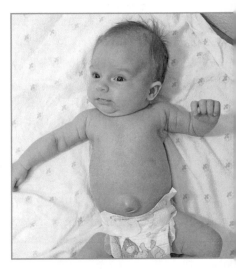

The muscles on your baby's stomach are very weak. When a bulge forms by the belly button, this is called an umbilical hernia.

should not be used. Time will almost always fix this problem.

For the few umbilical hernias that persist past three years of age, surgical repair may be necessary. In the very rare event that the area becomes red and painful to touch, seek medical attention immediately.

Caput Succedaneum

For a newborn, making one's way out of the birth canal is no small trick. The opening is not very wide and most babies lead the way head first. Every time mom attempts to push the baby out, his small head is being pushed against her pelvic bone. Frequently, swelling of the scalp will occur. This is called caput succedaneum.

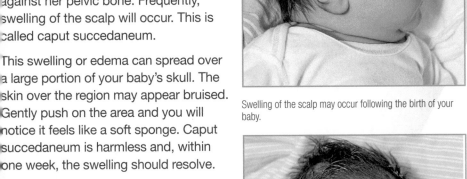

This swelling or edema can spread over a large portion of your baby's skull. The skin over the region may appear bruised. Gently push on the area and you will notice it feels like a soft sponge. Caput succedaneum is harmless and, within one week, the swelling should resolve.

Swelling of the scalp may occur following the birth of your baby.

Sometimes a larger, more firm swelling will occur on the scalp, often increasing in size during the first two or three days of life. His skin will appear normal, but the swelling will be confined to one area and will have a very clear border. Ask your baby's physician if this is a cephalohematoma. If it is, this is almost always harmless and was caused by some bleeding under the scalp that occurred as your baby was pushing his way into the world.

Depending on the cause, scalp swelling can take up to twelve weeks to fully resolve.

Celphalohematomas can take up to twelve weeks to fully resolve. Most heal without a problem, but rarely a localized infection may form at the site. If the swelling is very large, your baby may be at a higher risk for jaundice or anemia. Your baby's physician will decide if further evaluation is necessary.

Notes

Chapter 6

The Sick Baby

When to be Concerned.

Unless you keep your baby in a bubble, she will eventually catch a cold or develop a fever. Understanding what to expect and what to watch for should ease your concerns. Only the most common problems are discussed here. When in doubt about your child's health, talk to your baby's physician.

• •

Common Cold

It's a beautiful day outside and you might feel wonderful if your little one didn't have a green, runny nose. You know it must be bronchitis because his persistent cough is rattling the house, your neighbor's child has the same thing and their doctor prescribed an antibiotic for their child. Before yelling at the poor person who tells you this is a simple cold needing only comfort care, let's review the life cycle of a common cold.

An average cold can last ten days. Typically, a child will start with a clear runny nose, a mild nighttime or early morning cough and possibly a mild sore throat. After three or four days, the nasal secretions will thicken and become greenish-yellow in color. Your child may develop a low-grade fever up to 102.0 degrees Fahrenheit (38.9 degrees Celsius).

Usually, your child's cold will start with a clear runny nose, a mild nighttime or early morning cough and possibly a sore throat. The average cold can last for ten days.

At this point, if you are going to run anywhere, make it to your medicine cabinet for a nasal suction bulb and an appropriate fever medication. Your baby's doctor should be consulted about proper dosing of acetaminophen for babies younger than six months of age. Seeking medical advice is especially important if your baby is younger than three months of age and has a fever because, as discussed under Fever on page 57, a fever may be a sign of a more serious illness. Ibuprofen or acetaminophen are good choices for reducing a low-grade fever in babies six months of age or older. A box of tissues or a soft rubber suction bulb does wonders for clearing your baby's nose. A humidifier can help comfort mild throat irritation. Chances are, after four days of a thick greenish-yellow runny nose, the nighttime and early morning cough may worsen a little, but those yucky secretions will clear and all should be well within a few days.

At this point, if you are going to run anywhere, make it to your medicine cabinet for a nasal suction bulb and an appropriate fever medication.

Yes, a common cold will last seven to ten days, three days of low-grade fever is normal and green mucus does not necessarily need to be treated with an antibiotic. Remember that the average child gets sick five to eight times each year. So, when should you worry?

If your baby has trouble breathing, he should immediately be seen by a physician. Also, any baby younger than three months of age should be seen immediately by your baby's physician.

Common colds last seven to ten days. Three days of a low-grade fever is normal. And green mucus doesn't necessarily need antibiotics for treatment.

Other reasons to visit a doctor include a possible ear ache, high fever (over 102.0 degrees Fahrenheit or 38.9 degrees Celsius), fever for more than three days, greenish-yellow runny nose for more than four days, or cold symptoms lasting more than ten days. Finally, if you are still worried about your baby, call the doctor. It's better for you to be told that only tender loving care is necessary rather than risk a sleepless night worrying about your little one.

Nasal Suctioning

Babies are nose breathers. If they cannot breathe through their nose, babies don't eat or sleep well, which means you won't sleep well. I would love to hand your baby a tissue and tell him to blow, but I doubt he'll listen. That's why suctioning his nose becomes the most reasonable option.

When is it necessary to suction the nose? Watch your baby trying to latch onto a nipple, bottle or pacifier. If his nose is too clogged and this inhibits breathing while

Mixing Nasal Saline Solution

Mix 1 cup tap water with 1/4 teaspoon table salt (250 milliliters tap water with 1.25 milliliters table salt).

Stir and pour into a squirt bottle.

Fresh solution should be made daily.

atching on, it's time to get out the nasal suction bulb.

Before suctioning the nose, gather the necessary items. You will need a nasal suction bulb, tissues and nasal saline solution. It really helps if someone is there to help you hold your baby.

Position your baby on his back with his arms to the side. If you are right-handed, positioning his head to the left is easiest for nasal suctioning. Lefties should do the opposite. Cover one of his nostrils with your finger to prevent air from getting through and give one large squirt of nasal saline solution into the uncovered nostril using a small squirt bottle. While keeping one nostril plugged with your finger, quickly squeeze air out of the nasal suction bulb, insert the tip gently but firmly into the nostril where the saline was applied and release pressure from the bulb. All of the saline and nasal secretions should be drawn into the bulb with ease. Squirt the contents of the bulb onto some excess tissue and suction

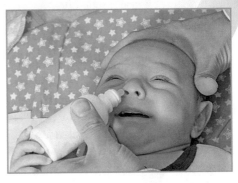

Cover one of his nostrils with your finger to prevent air from getting through and give one large squirt of nasal saline solution into the uncovered nostril.

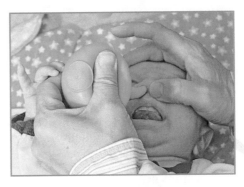

Keep one nostril plugged with your finger, quickly squeeze air out of the nasal suction bulb, insert the tip gently but firmly into the nostril where the saline was applied and release pressure from the bulb.

again. Use more saline if the secretions are very thick and are not yet coming out easily. Do not be timid. A big squirt of saline is safe to use. Wipe the nose with tissue as needed to remove excess secretions. It should take two to four suctions to clear his nostril. You will know when his nose is clear because the suction bulb will quickly inflate when released and he will breathe easier. Once air is flowing well through the nostril, do the same to the other side. He might seem uncomfortable at first, but don't worry. He will quickly become happy once he realizes he can breathe more easily.

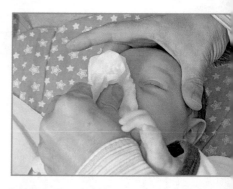

Squirt the contents of the bulb onto some excess tissue and suction again. Use more saline if the secretions are very thic and are not yet coming out easily. Wipe the nose with tissue remove excess secretions.

Sometimes, when his nose is very inflamed from a cold, a small amount of bleeding may occur, or it may come out when you suction his nose. This is harmless (really!) and you may continue to suction until the nose is clear. In the very rare instance that the nose continues to bleed, stop suctioning and gently pinch his nose until the bleeding stops. Call your baby's physician to discuss alternate methods of making your baby comfortable.

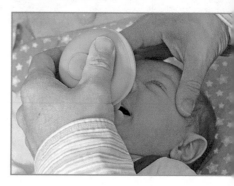

It should take two to four suctions to clear his nostril. His nose is clear when the suction bulb quickly inflates when it's released and he breathes easier. Once air is flowing well through the nostril, do the same to the other side.

Nasal suctioning should be reserved for instances when your baby is very uncomfortable because of the stuffed nose. You may suction as often as necessary, although before feeding and before bedtime will be most helpful in making your baby feel better. It is safe to suction his nose at any age, but from a practical standpoint, after his first birthday, the task is difficult and the benefit is minimal. Most children older than one year old are more comfortable breathing through their mouth for a few days until symptoms of the common cold resolve.

Fever

A fever is harmless. Fevers will not cause brain injury. A baby's high temperature is her body's attempt to fight infection. Although the fever is harmless, the underlying infection may be serious. Before we discuss how to determine the seriousness of the underlying infection, we must first define fever.

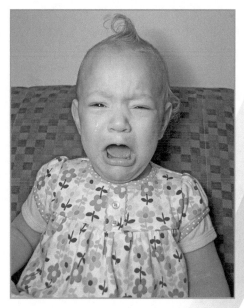

A baby's high temperature is her body's attempt to fight infection.

The days of mercury thermometers are gone. This is a new world and there are many ways to take your child's temperature. So how do you choose between oral, ear, axillary (armpit) or rectal thermometers? Although rectal thermometers are the most accurate, rarely is it necessary to be so precise. If your baby has not eaten recently, oral thermometers are probably sufficient, but getting a temperature from the armpit is the easiest method and is accurate enough. Make certain her armpit is dry. If your baby is overdressed, undress her for a few minutes before taking her axillary temperature. A newborn's ears are so small, I advise against using the ear thermometers. As you can see from the box, how a fever is defined depends on how it was taken.

Definition of Fever

Rectal ≥ 100.4 degrees Fahrenheit (38.0 degrees Celsius)

Axillary ≥ 99.0 degrees Fahrenheit (37.2 degrees Celsius)

Oral ≥ 100.0 degrees Fahrenheit (37.8 degrees Celsius)

Ear ≥ 100.4 degrees Fahrenheit (38.0 degrees Celsius)

Besides measuring your baby's temperature to evaluate how sick she is, you can sometimes determine which direction her fever will go within the next hour. If your baby feels cold and clammy, all the blood vessels in her extremities have become smaller and her fever is probably still climbing. Heat is being retained by the body. Anything you do to bring down the temperature on a clammy child experiencing chills is probably not going to help. If, instead, your baby feels very hot and is "burning up," the blood vessels have opened and your baby is now releasing heat off the body. In a short time, her temperature is likely to go down, even if you do nothing.

Now that we understand fevers, when should you worry? For babies younger than three months of age, any fever in your little one deserves a phone call to your baby's doctor. Because newborns do not have many ways of letting us know they are ill, it is best to be cautious. Sick babies do not eat, rarely urinate, become extremely irritable and often develop a fever. If the temperature is high, talk to your newborn's physician.

Although the fever is harmless, the underlying infection may be serious.

Once a baby is older than three months of age, fevers become less of a concern. This is because your baby is now interacting more and can give you a few more clues as to how she feels. Fever-reducing medicines are safe to use. Acetaminophen is the preferred choice for children younger than six months of age. Older children can safely use ibuprofen or acetaminophen. Consult your child's physician about dosing.

Stick with one fever-reducing medicine only to avoid the risk of overdosing. There is no need to alternate medicines. Also, never give aspirin to a child because aspirin can cause a deadly

After a few hours of fever, the temperature should come down and your baby should perk up. If between episodes of fever your baby interacts normally, this is reassuring.

disease in children called Reye's Syndrome. Cool baths are unnecessary. Instead, sponge lukewarm water on your baby. When the water evaporates off your baby's body, she will feel cooler. Do not use cold water. The goal is to soothe your baby.

When your older baby has a fever, how do we know if the underlying infection is dangerous? It is time to take another close look at your baby.

After a few hours of fever, the temperature should come down and your baby should perk up. If between episodes of fever your baby interacts normally, this is reassuring. Really sick children almost always look ill even when the fever breaks.

Do not be surprised if the fever goes up again within a few hours and your baby wishes to sleep. When she is ill, her fever will often come and go, and it can last up to three days. As long as your child has intervals of appearing perky and normal, it's safe to watch and wait.

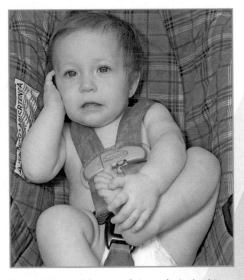

Fever-reducing medicines are safe to use. Acetaminophen is the preferred choice for children younger than six months of age. Older children can safely use ibuprofen or acetaminophen. Talk to your child's doctor about the needed dosage.

When should you consult your baby's doctor? If your baby seems persistently less alert than normal, does not wake up to eat or drink and/or seems lethargic, floppy or irritable, immediate medical attention is necessary. Unusual rashes should also be evaluated promptly. Fever associated with diarrhea or vomiting is also a reason for concern in little children. Babies are small and if they don't get enough to drink, they are at risk for dehydration. Fewer than two wet diapers during daylight hours is abnormal and deserves a physician's evaluation for signs of dehydration. Although difficult to determine in a young baby, always question if there is tummy

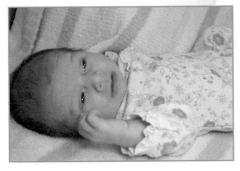

For babies younger than three months of age, any fever in your little one deserves a phone call to your baby's doctor.

pain, ear discomfort, a sore throat or pain when urinating. Any of these concerns deserve prompt medical attention.

Finally, always call if you are concerned. Your baby's physician should be available to assess and reassure. Concerned parents should never hesitate to call. A quick conversation might be all that is necessary to put you at ease.

Urinating

Knowing how many wet diapers your baby makes during the day is an easy way to tell if he is drinking enough fluids. For healthy newborns (please see Feeding on page 62), expect the number of wet diapers to increase daily until one week of age when a newborn should be producing six to eight wet diapers per day.

When a baby is older, the number of diapers will vary. At least two wet diapers per daylight hours is reassuring. Anything less should make you question if your baby is getting enough to drink. If your little one looks ill or has a fever, and is not urinating at least twice a day, it's time to speak with your baby's doctor.

Notes

Chapter 7

Since You Asked

Simple Answers to Common Questions.

My list of lectures is short. The reason is simple. There are many ways to raise a child, few of which are wrong. If your method is working for you, chances are my view is useless.

Just the same, I have my views and I enjoy anticipating and correcting problems before they arise. If you wish to avoid problems and are experiencing difficulty in one of these key areas, this advice should help. I guarantee my advice is appreciated by the majority of parents who bring their child to me. I also guarantee some will disagree with my views. Such is the nature of advice. When it is time to act, do what is in your heart, but remember, it's always best to be informed so you can make wise and informed decisions.

• •

States of a Baby

Before discussing key issues and how to solve them, it is important to understand your baby. Newborn babies live in one of four states: sleeping, calm, alert and crying. Once a baby is in a particular state, they tend to stay that way until an event prompts them out of it. This is why I often tell parents that a crying baby is a sign of a crying baby.

Do not read too much into crying. If your newborn was recently fed, the diaper is dry and you do not suspect a fever or illness, bundle your baby tight, sit comfortably in a quiet environment, gently rock her and feel comfortable knowing that it's okay your baby is crying. Once you create a soothing

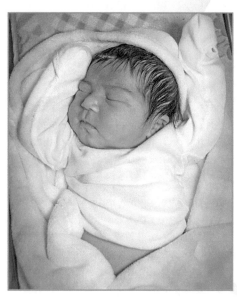

Newborn babies live in one of four states: sleeping, calm, alert and crying.

environment, your baby is likely to slip back into a state of calm. This may take twenty minutes, but no harm is done. Your baby is allowed to cry.

After a period of calm, do not be surprised if a loud noise or some other external event prompts your baby back into crying. Remember from the Development chapter, crying is one of the results of the startle reflex so there is no need to worry. Make certain your baby is well-bundled and re-establish a calm environment. Before long, your newborn will learn to calm himself with ease.

Feeding

If ever there was a subject with too many opinions, this is one of them. Fortunately, nearly all advice works for the simple reason that at four months of age, your baby will figure things out and regulate himself. Until then, this is what I advise.

Almost all feeding advice will work because by four months of age, your baby will figure things out and regulate herself.

Newborns rarely start out as vigorous eaters. If you choose to breast-feed, this is not the time to introduce formula. Attempt to breast-feed for up to ten minutes on each side (fifteen minutes maximum per side) every two to three hours. At night, five-hour stretches are reasonable should your newborn wish to sleep. Be sure to allow at least two hours between feedings (from finish to start). If your baby is not interested, wait until the next feeding. If two feedings pass without interest, inform your baby's doctor.

Breast milk can be refrigerated for up to two weeks and frozen for up to two months. Once out of the refrigerator, your milk will be good for six hours.

Why do I set limitations on duration and feeding intervals? It's for two reasons. First, you are not a pacifier. Babies will suck for long periods of time because it is a reflex action. It is a useful reflex, but a reflex just the same. The Development section on page 7 demonstrates the sucking reflex nicely. For those who say you cannot overstuff a breast-fed baby, explain to me how a mom with twins can sufficiently breast-feed both children? Babies can be overstuffed. Besides, do you really want to spend the next six to twelve months with sore nipples?

Second, all of us need time to digest our meal. After eating, everything sits in the stomach for about an hour and is broken down to aid absorption into our body. Then food is released from the stomach and moves through the rest of our intestines. Many babies squirm at this point. The reason for seeming uncomfortable is beyond me, but that is how they appear. The first response by most parents is to calm their newborn by feeding him again. At first, this solution seems to work great. Food goes back into the stomach, the digestive process starts over again, and the previous meal is halted in its journey through the intestines. Miraculously, your baby is calm again. Unfortunately, you have stopped the digestive process midstream. In an hour, food starts moving through the system, your baby gets fussy again, and the vicious cycle of feeding to calm continues. Within a week your baby is fussy, colicky, gassy and overstuffed. Much of this can be avoided if feeding intervals are extended just a little. Try allowing a minimum of two hours to pass between feedings. I think you will be happier and so will your baby.

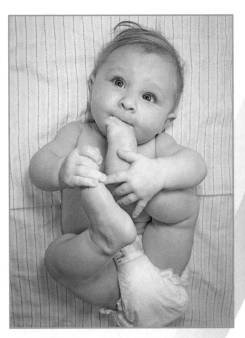

Babies will suck for long periods of time because it is a reflex action. It is a useful reflex, but a reflex just the same.

For bottle-fed babies, the same principles apply. During the first forty-eight hours of life a baby should not eat more than one-half to one ounce (15 to 30 milliliters). Babies' stomachs are still very small and should not be overstretched with food. Within one week, he should be taking two to three ounces (60 to 90 milliliters) of formula every two to three hours. More than three ounces (90 milliliters) and you are on the road to that vicious cycle

Typically babies lose up to eight percent of their birth weight by one week of age and regain this weight by two weeks of age. For a baby weighing eight pounds (3.6 kilograms) this is about ten ounces (280 grams) of weight loss.

I mentioned earlier. At two months of age, increase the volume to four ounces (120 milliliters). After four months of age, restrictions are unnecessary. Babies will regulate themselves with ease.

When you first start feeding your newborn, how do you know your baby is getting enough to eat? Two things will be evident. First, if breast-feeding, your breasts will soon feel firm and uncomfortable (usually after two to four days from the onset of breast-feeding). Congratulations, your milk is in. Second, the number of wet diapers will increase. Count the number of wet diapers. They are coming from somewhere. Forget about the soiled diapers. It is the wet ones that matter.

Expect the following. On day one of life, one wet diaper. On day two of life, two wet diapers. An additional wet diaper will be made each day until one week of age when your baby should be producing six to eight wet diapers per day. In the rare instance that the number of wet diapers is not increasing, it is time to see your baby's doctor. A quick weight check will help determine if there is a problem. Another sign that your milk production may be insufficient is the appearance of the brick-red urate crystals after four days of life as discussed on page 41.

After four months of age, restrictions are unnecessary. Babies will regulate themselves with ease.

It's time to have your baby weighed. What about the weight? Why is your baby losing weight during the first few days of life? This is because it takes a few days for you to have sufficient milk supply to satisfy your baby. Yes, your baby is hungry at first. But if he does not work a little, how is he going to stimulate your milk supply?

Ask your baby's doctor if supplementing with vitamin D or fluoride are necessary.

Typically babies lose up to eight percent of their birth weight by one week of age and regain this weight by two weeks of age. For a baby weighing eight pounds (3.6 kilograms) this is about ten ounces (280 grams) of weight loss. Conversely, a baby who is one pound above birth weight by two weeks of age is probably being overstuffed. Should colic begin, think about this.

To recap, your baby will not eat much during the first forty-eight hours of life. By one week of age, breast-feed for five to ten minutes on each breast or give two to three ounces (60 to 90 milliliters) from a bottle every two to three hours (up to five hour intervals at night). At two months of age, increase the volume to four ounces (120 milliliters). By four months of age, let your baby set the pace and volume for feeding.

When it comes to introducing solids, there are no set rules. At four months of age, your baby's weight will have doubled and he is ready to try new things. I suggest starting with rice cereal. Mix one tablespoon of cereal with breast milk or formula and feed him the rice cereal with a spoon. The amount your baby eats is of little concern. This should be fun and the rice cereal is not intended to replace a feeding. It will also not make your baby sleep better at night despite what grandma tells you. By six months of age, all foods are fair game except for eggs, nuts, shellfish, strawberries and honey. Juice is fine to introduce at this point too, although I suggest limiting juice to six ounces (180 milliliters) per day because of the high sugar content. At one year of age, his weight will have tripled from birth and all foods are safe to introduce.

By six months of age, all foods are fair game except for eggs, nuts, shellfish, strawberries and honey.

Do not be surprised if the list of food "dos and don'ts" varies from physician to physician. This is because (with the exception of avoiding raw honey for the first year of life due to the risk of infantile botulism), there is no set science on introducing foods. However, definitely avoid anything that is cork-sized or appears to be a choking hazard. Have fun with feedings and do not over-think the process. Introducing one new food each week for fear of allergies is not necessary. Food allergies are infrequent and if a rash should appear, there is ample time

Avoid anything that is a cork-sized or appears to be a choking hazard.

to hold solids and determine the cause by a slow reintroduction of food. Before trying to determine the possible cause of a suspected food allergy, speak with your baby's physician about how best to proceed. Feeding should be enjoyable, not a chore.

Sleeping

Babies sleep more than your average teenager. Bundle your baby and place her in a crib with a firm mattress. To reduce the risk of Sudden Infant Death Syndrome, your newborn should be positioned on her back. Blankets and pillows can pose a hazard and are rarely necessary before one year of age.

A well-bundled baby will sleep for hours. Enjoy the quiet. You will need some rest for when your child is older. If your baby wakes every few hours, appears alert when awake, and eats at regular intervals, sleeping at all other times is normal. Should your newborn never seem to wake and always refuses to eat, speak with your baby's doctor.

A well-bundled baby will sleep for hours. Enjoy the quiet. You will need some rest for when your child is older.

Keeping your baby warm can be accomplished easily without a blanket. Count how many layers of clothing you are wearing to be comfortable in your current setting and add one additional layer to your baby. Most often, pajamas and a swaddling blanket will be sufficient. There is no need to overbundle your baby.

Although I am a big fan of schedules, most babies are not. Newborns seem to mix up day and night. With patience, your baby is likely to follow a pattern of two nighttime feedings, typically at around midnight and three in the morning. By two months of age, start discouraging the three o'clock feeding. This is often easily accomplished by allowing your baby to fuss at three in the morning. Should your little one start crying, attend to her needs and feed your baby if necessary. Although midnight to sunrise without feedings is a realistic goal for a two-month-old baby, do not worry if she has other plans. For now, let your baby be in control.

Four months of age is an ideal time to set limits and encourage nighttime sleep. Between eight at night and sunrise, feeding is not necessary. Also, unless you wish your child to be in bed with you when she is three years old, now is the time to move her into a separate room. Why now? It's time to discuss development.

Within the next couple of months your newborn will reach a developmental milestone called object permanence. At four months of age, when an object is out of sight, to your baby, it does not exist. Try removing a toy from the hand of your four-month-old baby and hiding it under a blanket. Your baby will not yet know to reach under the blanket to find the missing object.

Similarly, if your baby is allowed to sleep in her own room, she will wake at night and amuse herself without demanding your attention for playtime. If you are not in sight, she will not search for you.

Once object permanence is established, life is not so simple. Upon waking, your child knows you are close by and that you are a sucker. Even though you are out of sight, she knows you are close by. If she screams long enough, you will come. Face it, she is using you.

Establishing the ideal sleep pattern before object permanence sets in increases the likelihood of your baby maintaining the desired sleep pattern once she learns how to manipulate you. If you allow her to amuse herself,

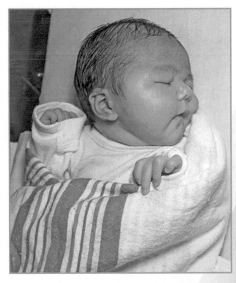

To reduce the risk of Sudden Infant Death Syndrome, place your baby to sleep on her back.

she will maintain the familiar pattern that has been established. If having her own room is not an option, the same principle still applies. When she awakes, leave her alone. The middle of the night is not the time for a play session. Whether she is in your room, with a sibling, or in her own room, your baby must learn to soothe herself.

Four months of age is an ideal time to set limits and encourage nighttime sleep. Also, unless you wish your child to be in bed with you when she is three years old, now is the time to move her into a separate room.

If she is not hungry, why is your baby waking up at night? Your baby has a secret that you do not yet know. Babies do not sleep all night long. In the best of worlds, a baby will awake, amuse herself, and put herself back to sleep. If you turn off the baby monitor - and you should - you will not ever know about such nighttime awakenings.

The most ideal sleeping pattern is achieved when parents learn to leave a fussy baby alone. If she is making soft noises and moving around, allow your baby to soothe herself. If she is screaming, make certain she is not hurt and then try to calm her without picking up your baby. Definitely avoid nighttime feeding at this age. Reintroducing food at night will create a very difficult habit to break. Periodically, you may have a few long nights, but this is much preferred to the nightly calming sessions you will be hosting should you not allow your baby to become a good self-soother.

Colic

If you follow my advice on feeding and sleeping, your baby might still get colic. There is no great explanation for colic. There is also no great remedy for colic. Before discussing how to make life easier during this unpleasant phase, let's define colic.

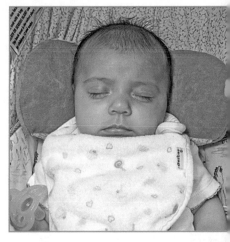

Setting your baby's sleep pattern before object permanence sets in increases her ability to become a self-soother, and gains you some sleep in the process!

The textbook definition for colic is prolonged periods of crying, multiple times a week, in an otherwise healthy baby. A nurse once explained it to me as follows: The baby who is a dream in the hospital will cry one to two hours per day during the first couple of months and up to four hours per day by three months of age. At four months of age, colic passes and all is well. I also remind parents that by nine months of age your baby will be mobile and life as you know it will be over. You will be much too busy trying to keep up with your baby to wonder why he isn't crying anymore.

Colic is defined as prolonged periods of crying, several times a week, in an otherwise healthy baby.

Before labeling every crying spell in your newborn's life as colic, it's important to make sure that a more significant problem hasn't been missed. Review the basics. Is your baby hungry? If your baby was fed within the last hour, the answer is

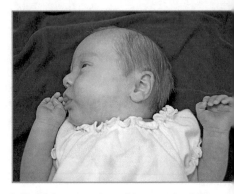

Before labeling every crying spell in your newborn's life as colic, make sure that a more significant problem hasn't been missed.

probably no. Is his diaper wet or soiled, requiring a change? Assuming basic needs have been met, think for a moment about the unlikely causes.

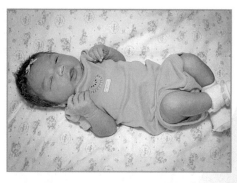

Reassure yourself that your baby is not ill. Does your baby feel feverish? Does he seem lethargic or have a weak cry? Have the number of wet diapers decreased in the past day or two? Did a hair get wrapped around his finger, toe or penis? I am always amazed how a first-time parent has the ability to sense when their newborn is ill. If you feel strongly about your concerns, do not dismiss them. Discuss these issues with your baby's physician.

Having reassured yourself the crying is from colic, keep the expected pattern in mind. Colic typically begins around two weeks of age and reaches a peak before three months of age.

If none of the above is evident, chances are this is colic. So, what should you do? The goal is simple. Transition your baby from a crying state to a calm state. Now is the time to review States of a Baby on page 61. Create a soothing, calm environment and play some pleasant music. Swaddle your baby tight, get comfortable in a rocking chair, offer your baby a pacifier and gently rock him until he calms. Most babies will relax within twenty minutes. If you are feeling very stressed by these bouts of crying, leave your baby swaddled in a crib and walk to a quieter place in the house for five minutes to allow yourself to relax. If you still feel very stressed, speak with your baby's physician.

For the few babies who do not calm, finding a solution becomes more difficult. If calming does not work, other interventions will likely fail too. Baby formulas are rarely the problem and switching formula is rarely the solution. True milk allergies are extremely uncommon and are usually associated with poor weight gain, abdominal bloating, diarrhea and blood in the stool. It's a rare instance when reflux can be so severe that it is painful. If your baby vomits forcefully and appears extremely uncomfortable, speak with your baby's doctor. Over-the-counter remedies are also useless. They have not been proven to help. Save your money. Chances are your baby just needs to cry.

Having reassured yourself the crying is from colic, keep the expected pattern in mind. Colic typically begins around two weeks of age and reaches a peak before three months of age. Coincidently, babies often poop less frequently starting at six weeks of age, but this is normal and should not be painful. Evening clusters of crying are most common. Before you know it, four months will have passed and your baby's colic should be resolved.

Pacifiers

Why some people are opposed to pacifiers is a mystery to me. The sucking reflex (see Development on page 7) is a powerful instinct in babies. Between feedings, a baby will remain quiet and content for hours if she is permitted to suck on a pacifier.

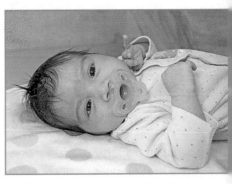

Pacifiers can be introduced on your baby's first day. This will help prevent you from becoming a human pacifier between feedings, and your newborn will quickly learn which nipple provides food. Your baby will not be confused.

Pacifiers can be introduced on your baby's first day. This helps prevent you from becoming a human pacifier between feedings.

Despite my adoration for pacifiers, keep a few points in mind. Pacifiers do not replace meals. Be aware of your newborn's feeding schedule. Never tether the pacifier to your baby's clothing. The cord can get caught around the neck and become a choking hazard. Finally, when your baby turns a year old, throw the pacifier away. Simply drop it in the trash can and do not look back. Within a few days your child will have forgotten about it and you will save a fortune in future orthodontic work. For the doubters out there, start looking at the teeth of toddlers. Look for the children who clench their teeth and can still stick a straw in their mouth through the gap created by prolonged pacifier sucking. Trust me - you want to lose the pacifier when your child turns one.

Hiccups

I have a personal theory about hiccups. Do not ask for proof because none exists. My view is from observation.

Babies are spitty. Food may not always come out of their mouths, but they still spit up a little. If this food makes its way to the windpipe, the airway becomes irritated and hiccups begin.

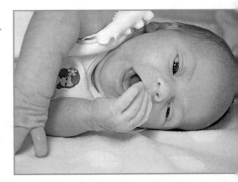

Most babies who get the hiccups also had hiccups while you were pregnant. There was nothing you could do about the hiccups then and there is nothing you need to do about the hiccups now. This mild nuisance will resolve itself with time. Besides, the hiccups probably bother us more than it bothers them.

Most babies who get the hiccups also had hiccups while you were pregnant. There was nothing you could do about the hiccups then and there is nothing you need to do about the hiccups now.

Teething

Drooling is a sign of drooling. Teeth usually appear between four months and one year of age. Teething is when you actually see the new tooth. Anything else you see is just a baby thing. They put their hands in their mouth, chew vigorously on their fists, and stimulate saliva production. Because of this, all the drool runs out of their mouth. This is just what babies do.

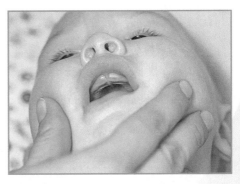

Teeth usually appear between four months and one year of age. Teething is when you actually see the new tooth.

When you see those two bottom teeth finally start to appear, you need to know that the eruption caused by the teeth pushing through her gums can be uncomfortable and may cause a low-grade fever, but nothing over 100.4 degrees Fahrenheit (38.0 degrees Celsius). A teething ring or pacifier is usually sufficient to soothe your baby. If your baby is older than six months and mildly irritable, some ibuprofen every six hours for one or two days is fine to use. Be cautious though, because the irritability may be a sign of illness and you do not want to overlook a problem that may require medical attention.

Do not apply numbing gels to the gums because the chemicals can be absorbed into your baby and can be toxic. Over-the-counter teething tablets are considered safe but are useless. I have concerns about introducing such substances to children and do not advise their use.

Traveling

Just because you have a new baby, do not feel trapped at home. It is easier to go out with a newborn than it will be when your baby is six months old. Unless someone is coughing on your baby, you have little to be concerned about. Bundle your baby appropriately and go out. Even airplane travel is safe

Unless someone is coughing on your baby, you have little to be concerned about. Bundle your baby appropriately and go out.

and very simple with a newborn. If possible, offer a pacifier or feed your baby via bottle or breast during take-off and landing to reduce the possibility of ear discomfort when the pressure changes. Enjoy the world with your baby. You will be much happier not feeling trapped inside.

The Newborn and Two-Year-Old

On some rare occasions, parents will share their experiences and my view of pediatrics is forever altered. This happened to me on the day I saw a particular parent who brought in her two children to me for the first time.

Before I explain, please do not be discouraged by the thought of having more than one child. Siblings are a blessing. Multiple children bring countless joy and shed a unique dimension to life. Should you choose to have more than one child, knowing what to expect should help you bring out the best among your family. Consider this a peek into the future in an effort to avoid problems. Now back to my encounter.

Multiple children bring countless joy and shed a unique dimension to life.

This mom brought in her two children, a one-year-old to be examined and a three-year-old along for the ride. After finishing my exam, I asked if she had any questions. She confided in me that she did not like her three-year-old. That statement made my jaw drop. Her feeling began shortly after her second child's birth. Had she known what to expect, such resentment could have been avoided. So what happened here?

When her second child was born, her little boy was two years old. For those who do not know, two-year-olds are all me, me, me and me. In their small minds, children this age can never receive enough attention. Mom was overwhelmed by the competition of her older child and reacted in a negative manner.

For children younger than eighteen months or siblings older than three years, adapting to a new baby is relatively straightforward. Jealousy will always be part of the picture, but children at such ages seem to adjust readily. Two-year-olds are unique.

When a new baby is introduced to a two-year-old, one of three things will happen: You may be lucky and the newborn will integrate with ease. This rarely happens. Alternately, your older child may display immediate displeasure. One child I saw pointed at her sibling and stated, "Baby Out!" No hidden feelings there! The most common response is positive interaction with the baby, with all the anger directed at the parents. Your two-year-old will likely hit more, scream more and become very defiant. All the attention in the world will not correct these behaviors. What is a parent to do?

First, you need to accept that the moment the newborn was introduced into this world, your older child's life changed. You cannot set back the clock. Second, you cannot make things equal. There are times when one child gets more attention than the other. Such is life.

For children younger than eighteen months old or siblings older than three years, adapting to a new baby is relatively straightforward. Two-year-olds are unique.

Here are some suggestions for dealing with these long-term frustrations. Politely discourage improper behavior. The baby gets tons of attention for using a pacifier and bottle. Should your older child try to mimic use of such objects, simply remove them and remind her that big children do not use such items. It's best to keep the word "no" out of the conversation. You got your point across by simply removing the object from reach.

At two years old, chances are your child is not yet potty-trained. If such is the case, forget about potty training for six months. Why should an older sibling use a toilet if the baby gets so much attention by having the diaper changed? Until potty training is her idea, it probably will not happen. It's time to stock up on diapers.

With time, your child will adjust to the new family dynamics, and you will be happier knowing you have done nothing wrong by introducing a sibling into this world.

For those times when your older child has a temper tantrum, simply walk away. Your two-year-old will do anything to get attention, even if such interactions are negative. Remember, when you scold your child, she has your full attention. She's won. Unless you need to remove your child from an unsafe situation, deal with inappropriate behaviors by walking away. If necessary, place your child in a safe environment and then walk away. Two minutes of isolation is sufficient to get your message across. Your goal is to communicate by depriving attention, not with words.

Once you have made your point with a brief period of isolation, it's fine to resume normal activity. Your objective is two-fold. First, be consistent. Inappropriate actions, such as sucking on a bottle, must be discouraged and inappropriate behaviors must be ignored. Second, accept that angry outbursts are your child's way of dealing with frustration. This is nothing personal. At this point, these are the coping skills that your older child possesses. With time, your child will adjust to the new family dynamics, and you will be happier knowing you have done nothing wrong by introducing a sibling into this world. Eventually, they will likely become best of friends, although probably not during the first year of your newborn's life.

Advice

Advice comes early and from everywhere. Friends, relatives, strangers, books, magazines - I really mean everywhere. Suggestions start rolling in long before the baby is born and quickly escalate once he's here.

Amazingly, despite the contradictions, there are few suggestions that are flat-out wrong. But the advice may be wrong for

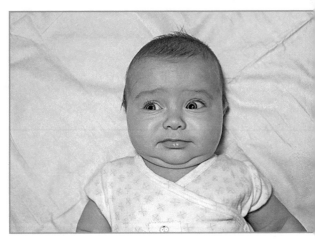

Advice comes early and from everywhere. The key to staying sane is to limit the sources of advice you take in and use your own common sense.

you. The key to staying sane is to limit the sources of advice you take in and use your own common sense.

If something is working for you, you don't need to change things. When problems arise, speak to your most trusted source first and follow their advice for a reasonable period of time. If you flip from suggestion to suggestion to suggestion, the outcome will be frustration without resolution.

Notes

Notes

Chapter 8

My Baby's Milestones

Follow Your Baby's Development.

Milestones are fun to watch and record. Keeping track of these major events creates memories that last forever. As you watch your baby develop, remember each newborn is different. Milestone ranges are approximate and babies progress as they wish. If your baby was born prematurely, these events may take even longer to achieve. Enjoy these moments and do not rush them. Your baby will be off to college before you can blink.

Baby's Name

Date of Birth

Birth Weight

Birth Height

Milestone	Typical Age Range	My Baby's First Events
Lifts head up momentarily	Birth to 6 weeks	
Smiles	Birth to 2 months	
Notices own hands	2 weeks to 4 months	
Laughs	1 month to 4 months	
Grasps a rattle	2 months to 4 months	
Brings own hands together	2 months to 4 months	
Squeals	2 months to 5 months	
Rolls over	3 months to 6 months	
Turns to parent's voice	3 months to 7 months	
Bears weight on legs when supported	3 months to 7 months	
Works for a toy	4 months to 6 months	
Passes an object from hand to hand	5 months to 7 months	
Sits without support	5 months to 9 months	
Makes the sounds "mama" or "dada"	5 months to 10 months	
Creeps on all four extremities	6 months to 9 months	
Grasps objects between the thumb and finger	7 months to 11 months	
Bangs two blocks together	7 months to 13 months	
Correctly says "mama" or "dada"	7 months to 14 months	
Waves bye-bye	7 months to 14 months	
Pulls to a stand	8 months to 10 months	
Stands alone	10 months to 14 months	
First word other than "mama" or "dada"	10 months to 16 months	
Walks well	11 months to 15 months	

Conclusion

Babies present many mysteries, not all of which can be answered among these pages. Hopefully I have shed some light on a few questions that have nagged at you but were never fully explained. When you know what to expect, development is a joy to watch, those peculiar rashes are no longer scary, and common problems are easily solved.

These pages have been written for you. My goal has been to answer the common questions that your baby's doctor does not have adequate time to explain. If you feel that there are gaps not addressed here, please share your questions with me at www.DrCareys.com. I welcome any suggestions for making this book more helpful for others. Hopefully what I have shared will bring you closer to your precious baby that you love so much. I wish that for you.

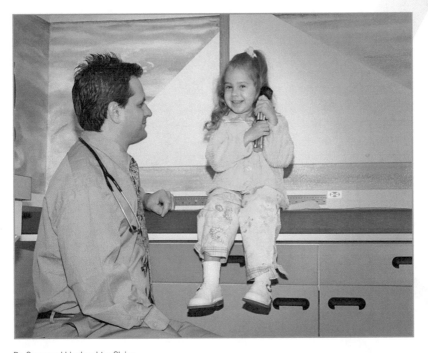

Dr. Carey and his daughter Claire.

Notes

Made in the USA
Columbia, SC
08 August 2024

40129472R00046